Spatial Portals
Gateways to Geographic Information

WINNIE TANG & JAN SELWOOD

ESRI Press, 380 New York Street, Redlands, California 92373-8100

Library of Congress Cataloging-in-Publication Data
Tang, Winnie.
    Spatial portals : gateways to geographic information / [authors, Winnie Tang and Jan Robert Selwood].—1st ed.
    p. cm.
    Includes bibliographical references.
    ISBN 1-58948-131-3 (pbk. : alk. paper)
    1. Geographic information systems. 2. Spatial analysis (Statistics) 3. Web portals. I. Selwood, Jan. II. Title.
G70.212T26 2005
910'.285—dc22   2005014321

Ask for ESRI Press titles at your local bookstore or order by calling 1-800-447-9778. You can also shop online at *www.esri.com/esripress.* Outside the United States, contact your local ESRI distributor.

ESRI Press titles are distributed to the trade by the following:

In North America, South America, Asia, and Australia:

Independent Publishers Group (IPG)

Telephone (United States): 1-800-888-4741

Telephone (international): 312-337-0747

E-mail: *frontdesk@ipgbook.com*

In the United Kingdom, Europe, and the Middle East:

Transatlantic Publishers Group Ltd.

Telephone: 44 20 8849 8013

Fax: 44 20 8849 5556

E-mail: *transatlantic.publishers@regusnet.com*

Book design by Jennifer Galloway
Book production and illustration by Jennifer Jennings
Cover design by Jennifer Jennings
Copyediting by Kandy Lockard
Print production by Cliff Crabbe

Spatial Portals

Gateways to Geographic Information

Contents

Foreword

Spatial data infrastructure is increasingly part of our world as more and more countries, organizations, and industrial associations create some form of SDI. We can see the most obvious SDI successes in the creation of Web-based metadata services that provide information about the data that users need. The U.S. Federal Geographic Data Committee Clearinghouse Registry, for example, lists nearly 300 registered users worldwide *(registry.gsdi.org/serverstatus)*.

Within the context of SDI, the development of spatial portals opens up new possibilities for Web-based metadata and application services. As their name suggests, spatial portals can be seen as gateways to geographic information (GI) resources. As such, portals provide points of entry to many SDI initiatives, helping Web users around the world find and connect to the richness of available GI resources. These portals also allow GI users and providers to share ideas, collaborate on content, and create consensus.

Spatial Portals, by Winnie Tang and Jan Selwood, is a valuable addition to GI and SDI literature that examines the opportunities and challenges associated with the construction and management of spatial portals in the SDI environment. More than that, *Spatial Portals* documents how this powerful technology links information providers to information users in ways that can save time, money, and even lives.

Ian Masser
Author of *GIS Worlds: Creating Spatial Data Infrastructures*

The developments described in the book you are about to read represent a milestone in the evolution of geographic information system (GIS) technology. I have spent the last 35 years of my professional life imagining a world where spatial portals would be a widespread reality—and here we are.

Today, we can access an almost unfathomable amount of geographic information captured from sensors and surveys, stored in spatial databases, and ultimately used by GIS applications and location-based services. An emerging spatial data infrastructure supports the dissemination of georeferenced information over the Internet. Innovations in GIS software, the World Wide Web, and other location-based information technologies are allowing for the creation of networks that serve up geographic information resources in new and exciting ways. Spatial portals—the subject of this timely text—are the gateways to this world of information. The Internet now offers thousands of Web sites that publish geographic information —from land records, census data, and utility infrastructure to vegetation maps, traffic patterns, and weather forecasts.

The term *spatial portals* describes a wide range of services and tools for accessing geographically referenced data. Depending on the end-user application and need, spatial portals are being deployed to serve up everything from driving directions and finished maps to raw geo-data and analytical models. In catalog form, searchable metadata creates loosely coupled or "federated" networks of resources. Networks of geographic knowledge allow people, organizations, and institutions to collaborate and share data and applications with one another and with the public. Spatial data infrastructure (SDI) projects are creating a policy framework which makes this possible for national and international initiatives and for individual organizations and industries.

Preface

Spatial portals connect service providers and users. They order and present vast quantities of information. They open avenues that lead to needed spatial information and then link directly to the source. As gateways, spatial portals are emerging as virtual meeting places that promote dialog, discussion, learning, and collaboration in the crucial spatial dimension. *Spatial Portals: Gateways to Geographic Information* highlights the successes and challenges of real-world spatial portals at work in different disciplines and organizations around the world.

It is my belief that this book will hasten the revolution already under way—a revolution in spatial data and spatial thinking that will provide humankind with a framework for solving our pressing problems as we move into the twenty-first century.

Jack Dangermond
President, ESRI

This book could not have been written without the support and help of many people who contributed their knowledge and insight to this developing field. We thank them all, and we are grateful for their generous contributions of time and energy, their enthusiasm and willingness to share, and their support of the aims of this book.

We particularly acknowledge the help of individuals in organizations around the world who found time in their busy schedules to contribute to individual chapters. At the Pacific Disaster Center, Dr. Allen Clark, executive director; Ray Shirkhodai, chief operating officer; Chris Chiesa, senior manager; and Nick Burk, technical editor, provided input and reviewed the description of PDC's portals. WorldSat International provided licensed mapping data. Hank Garie, executive director of Geospatial One-Stop, reviewed and provided helpful comments on the Geospatial One-Stop chapter. Roy Mellum, Norwegian Mapping Authority's (NMA) chief engineer and portal project manager, offered tremendous help with the preparation of the geoNorge portal chapter. Also at NMA, thanks to Olaf Østensen, technical director at NMA and chairman of ISO/TC211; Kåre Kyrkjeeide, director of the Arealis programme; and Anne Kirsten Stensby, chief county surveyor who reviewed and commented on the text. For the Transport Direct project, Nick Illsley, chief executive for Transport Direct and Paul Drummond kindly coordinated input and review of text and graphics for the Transport Direct chapter. Roy Laming, marketing director, and Chris Jackson, account manager at ESRI UK, also reviewed the chapter. Dwight McCullough, GIS coordinator for the Habitat and Enhancement Branch of Fisheries and Oceans Canada, Pacific Region, provided great help on the MAPSTER project. Thanks also to Chris North, director of technology and client support and

Acknowledgments

Heather Adams, communications specialist at ESRI Canada for their input and coordination on this chapter. At the South Carolina Department of Health and Environmental Control, thanks to the Division of Biostatistics and Health GIS that built the SCAN portal; Jared Shoultz, MA, informatics section manager, who helped draft the chapter; and the reviewers: Murray Hudson, director of PHSIS; Jim Ferguson, deputy director of PHSIS; Dr. Guang Zhao, director of the Division of Biostatistics and Health GIS; and Dr. Jeannie Eidson, GIS manager of the Bureau of Water. On the I2M chapter, Rich Grady, president of Applied Geographics, Inc., provided much assistance, as did his colleagues Patrick McHallam, Tom Harrington, and Peter Bujwid. Thanks to Jim Clayton, president of Unity Consultants; Capt. Mike Doyle, Public Works officer, U.S. Naval Academy; John Wyeth, Facilities Division head, Portsmouth Naval Shipyard; and Matt Davis, regional manager, ESRI Boston Office. The staff at Hong Kong Special Administrative Region Government's Planning Department Information Systems and Land Supply Section provided fast and helpful input for the GeoInfo One-Stop chapter. Thierry Gregorius, Global GIS/Spatial coordinator at Shell International Exploration and Production, B.V., provided input and valuable insight on implementing GIS portals in large corporations and Shell's spatial portals in particular. Also at Shell, Chucks Bisike-Ojiako, Geo-Information consultant, and Gerard Bosman, Geomatics Portfolio consultant, helped review the text; Kevin Mclay, Siti-Wana Gapar, and Sundaresan Ramamurthi provided screenshots of selected GIS uses in Oman, Brunei, and Europe, respectively.

At ESRI, many thanks to Marten Hogeweg for his patient explanations and reviews and to Anak Agung, Bernie Szukalski, Andrew Zolnai, Jeanne Foust, Kees van Loo, and

Bill Davenhall. Special thanks to Clint Brown, Mike Tait, David Maguire, and ESRI President Jack Dangermond, who generously spent time with us and shared their knowledge and vision. Pat Cummens from the ESRI Minneapolis office provided valuable input and assistance with the Geospatial One-Stop chapter. At ESRI China (Hong Kong), Paul Tsui, sales and marketing director, and Sallina Lee, senior system analyst, provided valuable input; Diana Ip helped with general administration; and Faheem Khan assisted in the search and coordination of graphic material. Thanks to Tasha Wade, Shelly Sommer, and the rest of the GIS Term Library staff for providing the glossary. Thanks to Mark Feduska for compiling the glossary terms, Pat Breslin for technical assistance, and all contributors who wrote definitions. We are most grateful to Professor Ian Masser, who wrote the foreword, and to Jack Dangermond, who wrote the preface.

At ESRI Press, Mark Henry patiently edited the text and shepherded it through production. Jennifer Jennings designed the cover and the book and brought order to the graphics. Jennifer Galloway provided invaluable advice. Thanks to Michael Hyatt for his expertise and wisdom, Christian Harder and Judy Hawkins for their enthusiastic support, Steve Hegle and Lesley Downie for their administrative support, and Cliff Crabbe, who oversaw print production. Thanks also to Kandy Lockard for her thorough copyedit. Many thanks to all.

CHAPTER I

Introduction

Spatial portals are Web sites that make it easier to find, access, and use geographic information available on the World Wide Web. They are changing the way we interact with spatial information and have the potential to become the fundamental platform through which we discover, publish, and share geographical knowledge.

These Web portals, or launch sites, are gateways to geographic information. They revolutionize the way we store, manage, find, share, and use knowledge about the world. Often the visible "front-end" of spatial data infrastructure (SDI), spatial portals allow us to access a network of information that spans the globe, discover information held by others, and present and share our own ideas, plans, and solutions.

In the computer industry, Web portals appeared as a means of indexing, ordering, and presenting an otherwise overwhelming mass of information. Typical examples are popular generic search portals, such as Google® or Yahoo!® that allow users to search against indexed catalogs of Web page content. A user arrives at the portal, enters a word or phrase, and the portal search engine matches this against an index of upwards of four or five billion possible Web pages to return a list of potentially relevant sites. These simple portal search sites have saved the Web from becoming irrevocably bogged down in a wealth of data and have played a significant role in the success and popularity of the Web.

Spatial portals are important because geospatial information is integral to the way we understand and respond to the world and events within it. We make many decisions based on proximity or coincidence. For example, traffic engineers might identify a certain road junction as dangerous because many accidents occur there. Store managers might choose the location of a new shop because many potential customers live in the area and there are no competing shops. Commuters may select a certain route home that both avoids traffic jams and takes them past a grocery store where they can shop on the way home. Because geospatial information is so fundamental, many different organizations use the same, or very similar, data. The engineer studying junction design, the store manager considering the new store, and the commuters plotting their route home all need an accurate map of the road network. Organizations and governments began implementing SDI to make common GI resources available starting in the early 1990s. Spatial portals make it easier to order, search, and access information on SDI.

Better, faster access to information leads to better-informed decisions and actions. Portals link information providers with information users. For example, portals can help in the aftermath of a natural disaster such as a large earthquake or typhoon. Successful response depends on the speed that rescuers can assemble accurate information on casualties, damage, and need and share this with the local, national, and international communities. Within hours of a disaster, a spatial portal can build a virtual project library from data and resources located all over the world—geological data from an oil exploration company; basic mapping, aerial imagery, and topographic data from national and international agencies; weather data from global weather services; fresh water points from a university research team; the location of landing sites, damage estimates, and current positions of medical teams from aid agencies and rescue teams. The portal allows organizations to pool information together, making it easily accessible to those that need it.

Or consider the process of evaluating proposals for a new power station, residential development, or airport. Planners, engineers, environmental consultants, legislators, local residents, and lobbying groups all need information to understand and evaluate the proposals. Through a spatial portal, each group searches and finds relevant information held by local, state, and federal agencies and other organizations. Better access to information fosters open debate, clearer understanding of the issues and options, and ultimately better decisions.

Spatial portals allow organizations to open their archives to the public. Space agencies, for example, can make terabytes of image data available to the public through a simple portal. Users can search the archives; locate and view images; check type, dates, and quality; perhaps even purchase and download data through the portal. They do this without leaving their desks, with the same ease and simplicity as if they held the information on their own desktop computers.

In each of these examples, spatial portals make it easier to share and access information, expand the range of information available, and reduce time and effort involved in finding it.

The importance of spatial portals is increasing as recent developments in geographic information systems (GIS) and the IT industry bring new challenges and opportunities.

New collection techniques create unprecedented volumes of data. Airborne and satellite imagery now map the world with submeter precision, location technologies track movements of objects and people within buildings, and real-time data feeds map minute fluctuations in traffic flow and air or water quality. Automation is improving the speed of data collection and dissemination. Organizations are replacing annual or monthly reports with real-time updates. The combination of speed and volume makes it increasingly inefficient, if not impossible, for many users to manage data on local desktops. Therefore, users will need to find and use geospatial information on very large, remote servers.

Data storage technology and networking are also progressing. New technologies, such as server clusters and grid computing, allow centralized server architectures to support large numbers of users. Networking technology, traditionally a major bottleneck in distributed computing, is evolving with the promise of wireless broadband and transfer speeds many times faster than those available today. Software for building applications makes it easier to exchange complex commands and data between remote applications. Web services, for example, now permit applications to work together across the World Wide Web, allowing users in Bolivia to find, view, update, analyze, and print data in computers in Hungary, Japan, or Canada. Geographic information systems are becoming networked, and spatial portals are the entry points, the gateways to such networked resources.

In response to the Indian Ocean tsunami of December 2004, the Pacific Disaster Center (PDC) *(www.pdc.org)* launched a portal providing news, data, and links to mapping services related to the disaster *(www.pdc.org/PDCNewsWebArticles/2004SouthAsiaTsunami/index.html)*. In addition, to support relief operations and the general public, the PDC launched the Southeast Asia and Indian Ocean Tsunami Response Map Viewer *(www.pdc.org/tsunami)* and underlying map service. This mapping application provides access to a wealth of high-resolution satellite imagery, damage maps, and other important geospatial information about impacted areas (see chapter 3 for another example on the value of spatial portals in the tsunami disaster relief efforts).

Based in Hawaii, the PDC fosters "disaster-resistant" communities through information, science, and technology in the Asia Pacific region and beyond. The center hosts a number of permanent portals aimed at improving coordination and access to information. The Asia Pacific Natural Hazards Information Network (APNHIN) *(apnhin.pdc.org)* helps disaster and resource managers, planners, governments, and nongovernmental organizations search for, evaluate, and access spatial information services relevant to hazard evaluation. The Network also assists in response planning and execution. Services registered at the APNHIN portal include online or downloadable datasets and applications. Users can combine text and map-based searches to find services covering a particular area, country, or topic.

The Asia Pacific Natural Hazards and Vulnerabilities Atlas *(atlas.pdc.org)* combines geographic and infrastructure data layers with historical and near real-time data on natural hazard events, including earthquakes, tsunamis, volcanic eruptions, and tropical storms.

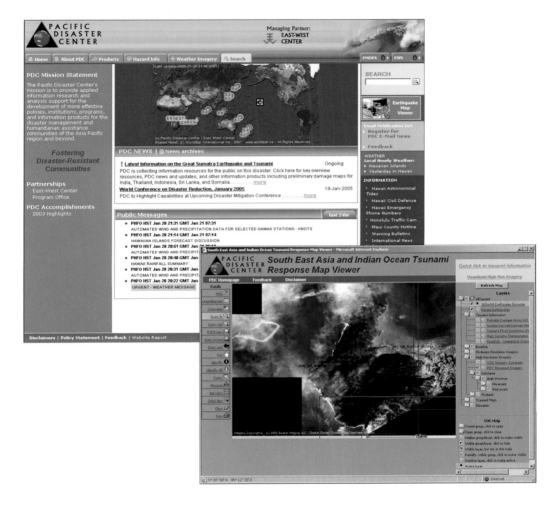

The Pacific Disaster Center *(www.pdc.org)* hosts a number of permanent portals that help governments, organizations, and the public search for, evaluate, and access spatial information services about natural hazards. The center's homepage, shown at top left, provides reports and location details about current natural hazards such as volcanic eruptions, typhoons, earthquakes, and tsunamis. The center also establishes dedicated portals in response to particular disasters. These help users quickly access specific event-related information. The image in the lower right shows the mapping portal launched in the aftermath of the powerful earthquake and devastating tsunami that hit many countries around the Indian Ocean in December 2004.

Courtesy of ©WorldSat International—All rights reserved.

Such developments bring new risks or heighten existing ones. Too much information can make locating relevant information more difficult and time consuming. Opening up archives and information resources, while increasing choice, can overwhelm users with data. Portals may reduce direct communication between information service providers and users. This makes it much harder for information providers to ensure that users are aware of the provenance, assumptions, and limitations of the services offered. Without this knowledge, there is a risk that users will misinterpret information or apply it incorrectly. Resources coming from different organizations may also be incompatible, using different formats or different ways to model or conceptualize real-world features that make it difficult, if not impossible, to integrate and use them together.

Many of these issues only appear as organizations start to design, construct, and use spatial portals. The experience gained from building and using spatial portals prompts new ways of describing and storing geospatial information, new ways to organize interfaces and tools that help users discover and search for information, and new ways to integrate and work with information services assembled from multiple organizations.

Spatial Portals: Gateways to Geographic Information is written against this background. Organizations large and small around the world already are demonstrating the great potential of spatial portal technology. However, challenging issues remain, and those providing and working with geospatial information are exploring different solutions. It is through this debate and implementing, testing, and monitoring results that best practice develops. With the exception of the following chapter that provides the background to the development of spatial portals and outlines their basic components, the rest of this book examines a collection of leading portal implementations. *Spatial Portals* illustrates the work of a number of pioneering projects drawn from a gamut of applications and disciplines.

The U.S. government's Geospatial One-Stop portal is the focus of chapter 3, which examines one of the most well-established national spatial data portals in the world. Chapter 4 looks at how the geoNorge portal in Norway not only promotes access and usage of data but also helps build a strong user community that works together to maintain and share mapping nationwide. Chapter 5 explores Transport Direct, an ambitious national travel information portal for the United Kingdom that forms an integral part of government's efforts to promote public transport and environmentally friendly travel. Chapter 6 focuses on the MAPSTER portal that helps the department of Fisheries and Oceans Canada in the Pacific Region disseminate data on the ecology and resources of the region's rivers and coastal waters. Designing spatial portals to disseminate sensitive and complex data is the subject of chapter 7, which examines South Carolina's Department of Health and Environmental Control's SCAN public health information portal. Chapters 8 looks at the use of portals in asset management and explores the U.S. Navy's I2M portal that tracks the condition of onshore naval facilities and facilitates review and processing of maintenance work. Chapter 9 focuses on the work of the Hong Kong Planning Department portal that promotes access to land-use zoning plans and planning application archives. Chapter 10 examines issues involved in developing portals in large global businesses with a look at how Royal Dutch Shell uses portal technology to manage and disseminate information within its Exploration and Production group.

In the afterword, we draw some lessons from the examples discussed in the book and look to future developments.

CHAPTER 2

Building spatial portals

Before looking at how organizations build and use spatial portals, it is helpful to explore the background of their development, their primary functions, and their types.

The development of portals

The computer industry adopted the word *portal* in the mid-1990s. Spatial portals are Web sites that either assemble many online resources and links into a single location to form easy-to-use products (such as America Online® or CompuServe®) or provide search tools that help users find information on the Web (for example, Yahoo! or Google). Derived from the medieval English word, *portle*, meaning city gate and originally from the Latin *porta* meaning simply gate, these sites aim to be their users' primary points of entry to the Web—their gateways, or portals. Web portals have proven extremely popular. As the number of users and the volume of content on the Web grew exponentially throughout the 1990s, portals provided a convenient way for the casual user to navigate what was otherwise rapidly becoming an impenetrable mass of information. Portals have played a significant role in the evolution and popularity of the Web by helping to connect Web users with Web content providers.

Demand from the geospatial information industry

Making connections between content providers and users is important for the geospatial information industry. As noted in chapter 1, many organizations often need the same geospatial information, whether maps of terrain, population distribution or habitat, place-name gazetteers (also called geographical dictionary databases), or collections of remotely sensed images. Organizations often share other forms of geospatial information: models for transport networks or for structuring survey results, and tools or processes to analyze geospatial data. The same route-finding tool can route ambulances for one organization, school buses for another, and delivery vans for yet another, and can work in towns and cities throughout the world. Improving how users find, access, and integrate information and how providers share their information with users is therefore of great relevance.

Starting in the 1960s, geographic information systems (GIS) technology revolutionized the way in which organizations create, analyze, and share geospatial information. GIS overcame the artificial separation between the map and textual attribute data by linking graphic data objects with relational databases. GIS technology made it easier to integrate, overlay, and analyze information coming from different sources. It also improved ways of distributing and sharing geospatial information. Users no longer had to go to map libraries to consult hardcopy maps or geographical dictionaries; they could bring digital data onto their own workstation and desktop computers, copy it on tape and disk, and (increasingly) share it across networks.

By the late 1980s and early 1990s, many governments and businesses had adopted GIS for these reasons. However, the geospatial community began to realize that barriers prevented it from fully accessing and sharing geospatial data. This was partly due to the success of GIS. As GIS became more accessible and easy to use, the number of organizations actively involved in creating and using spatial data grew dramatically, yet few standards governed the development of datasets. Differences in data models, nomenclature, and technology frustrated efforts to share and integrate data, models, and processes. The geospatial community had no consistent way of describing the source, quality, scale, intended use, and other basic details about information services. Users searching for information services often found it difficult to compare them or appreciate their intended use and limitations. As the number of users expanded, large data providers, such as national mapping agencies, had to spend more and more time explaining datasets, responding to requests for data, and circulating updates. Keeping data up to date and consistent became an increasingly time-consuming task for data provider and user alike.

Various governments have investigated handling and use of geographic information. Studies include those conducted by the Canadian government, 1986; the British government, 1987; the National Research Council in the United States, 1990; the Dutch government, 1995; and Australia and New Zealand, 1996. The studies revealed extensive fragmentation of geographic data and services between different departments, the inefficiencies and costs this entailed, and the need to improve coordination and sharing of spatial information.

Studies by governments and organizations illustrated the extent of the problem worldwide. Though conducted independently, the studies identified similar conditions and arrived at similar conclusions. They found that GIS offered real benefits and opportunities to manage, analyze, and share information better. However, limited coordination between GIS projects resulted in duplicated and wasted effort and inefficient information management and distribution. This hampered realization of the full benefits of GIS.

These studies led to concerted efforts to improve access to and coordination of geographic information. Many national mapping organizations embarked on spatial data infrastructure (SDI) projects. SDI, a term first used in 1993 by the U.S. National Research Council (Mapping Sciences Committee, 1993), established the technology, policies, and human resources to ensure efficient access to up-to-date and consistent spatial information. SDI encouraged the agreement of new standards for data transfer, storage, and the description of information services (called metadata). Mapping organizations collected metadata (and sometimes the datasets as well) into dedicated data hubs, or clearinghouses. Connecting clearinghouses through the Web created networks or infrastructures that made it easier for users to find geospatial information. SDI projects appeared within large businesses, international agencies such as the United Nations, and local and national governments. By the mid-1990s, mapping agencies and organizations involved in geospatial industry were participating in major international SDI projects such as the Global Spatial Data Infrastructure (GSDI) *(www.gsdi.org)*, launched in 1996.

Metadata describes the content, quality, condition, origin, and other characteristics of information resources in a standard, structured format. Metadata for spatial datasets may include details about the subject matter; how, when, where, and by whom data was collected; accuracy, scale, projection, resolution, and guidance on suitable use; and so on. Metadata for a functional service may describe uses, who developed it, version number, development environment, and input and output parameters.

A number of metadata standards have emerged. In the United States, the Federal Geographic Data Committee (FGDC) established the influential Content Standard for Digital Metadata description in 1998. Other standards include the National Geospatial Data Framework (NGDF) in the United Kingdom, the Australia New Zealand Land Information Council's (ANZLIC) metadata guidelines, and the Japanese Japan Metadata Profile (JMP). In July 2003, the International Organization for Standardization's (ISO) geographic technical committee (ISO/TC211) agreed on international spatial metadata standard ISO19115. Many national and private organizations are now reviewing this standard, with their goal either to adopt it or make their systems compatible with it.

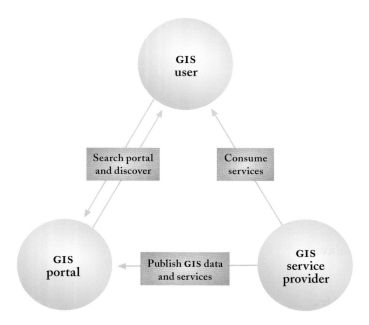

The relationship between spatial portals, users, and providers.

Spatial portals developed as the gateways to SDI initiatives and act as brokers between users and service providers. Information providers, whether individual agencies, private companies, or managers of a regional data hub, publish their services at the portals. Portals allow users to search and browse published services. If the user finds an interesting service, the portal then passes the user directly to the appropriate service provider. Users can access up-to-date, authorized information through a single location; service providers only need to update one location to reach many users.

Spatial portal functions

Spatial portals typically contain a number of common functions. As illustrated below, these include functions to search and discover services and provide news and other relevant information to the user community. Portals also offer administrative functions for service suppliers and users.

SERVICE SEARCH

- Spatial data
- Metadata search
- Structured interface

INFORM

- News/discussion forum
- Standards and cookbooks
- Thesauri and gazetteers

SERVICE DISCOVERY

- Metadata viewer
- Map viewer
- Link to content provider
- Connect to service
- Download service

ADMINISTRATION

- Catalog maintenance
- Harvesting
- Security
- User management
- Hardware/network support

Portals provide tools to search or find spatial information. The spatial search tools may display a map and allow users to define boundaries of an area of interest. A portal retrieves information services that cover the area of interest. Such functionality is helpful because describing the extent of an area of interest in words is often difficult. Other search techniques may allow users to select services by querying items within metadata records. For example, users could use fields such as keyword, place name, content description, service provider, scale, and key dates (date of creation, last update, and so on) to retrieve information. Users can often combine spatial searches with a range of parameters, allowing them to establish well-defined search criteria. Other approaches use the design of the portal interface to help users find information they need. Portals may collect information relevant to a particular topic into dedicated Web pages, or channels, or use nested legend-trees that help users navigate to increasingly detailed data layers.

In addition to search functionality, portals provide tools to view, explore, and download information services. Early spatial portals often only allowed users to view metadata. If users wished to use a service, the portal would link them to the relevant provider's Web site, where they could either download the service over the Internet or find contact details to arrange its delivery. However, many data and application services are now available as live Web services that users can work with directly online. Users can access these services through light Web-based mapping clients that the portal may provide from desktop GIS applications (thick clients). These tools allow users to combine, view, and work with multiple remote services over the Web. Depending on the type of portal, such mapping clients range from those providing relatively simple pan, zoom, and identify functionality to highly customized

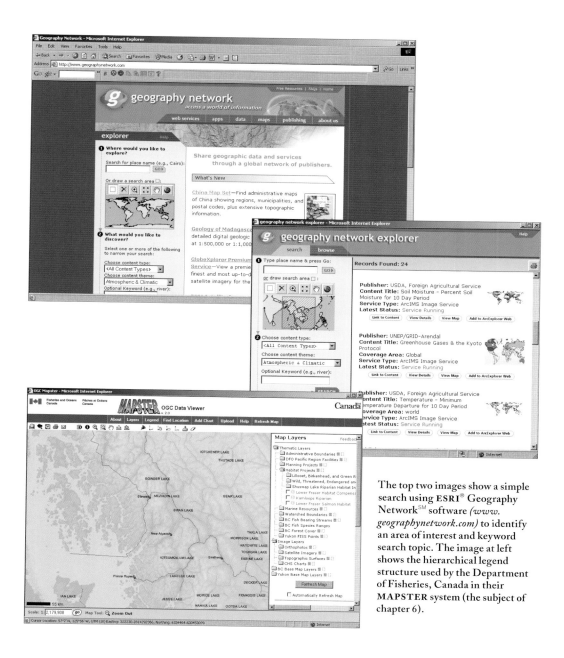

The top two images show a simple search using **ESRI**® Geography Network[SM] software *(www. geographynetwork.com)* to identify an area of interest and keyword search topic. The image at left shows the hierarchical legend structure used by the Department of Fisheries, Canada in their **MAPSTER** system (the subject of chapter 6).

mapping interfaces that permit focused query and analysis. If service providers charge for their information services, portals may also provide e-commerce and accounting functions that allow users to pay for services.

Portals also act as information and news centers. By providing common gateways, portals are convenient places to organize Internet forums or post briefing papers, news, draft standards, and other items of interest. The portal may provide additional information to help data providers or users understand or interpret standards such as thesauri or gazetteers.

Finally, portals contain administrative functions. These permit portal managers (and service providers) to add and update metadata, monitor usage and performance, and maintain the portal site. As users turn to spatial portals as the primary way to search and access resources, portals must remain available and provide reliable performance whenever needed. This often demands around-the-clock operation and robust disaster response planning to ensure smooth portal operation. User management functions allow managers to control access to all or part of the portal's contents.

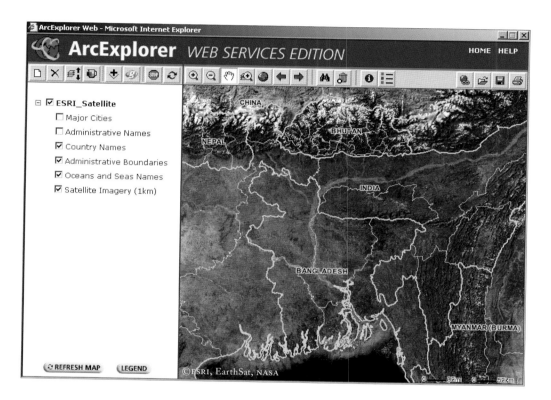

The Geography Network's ArcExplorer™ Web service allows users to add and overlay map services from multiple service providers and provides map navigation and query tools.

Types of spatial portals

Spatial portals are identified in three broad types: catalog portals, application portals, and enterprise portals. All facilitate access to geospatial information services, but they do so in different ways.

Catalog portals create and maintain indexes or "catalogs" describing available information services. Service providers create or place metadata on the portal. The portal arranges metadata records into a consistent, searchable catalog and allows user access. Users query the catalog based on metadata parameters. In most cases, the provider continues to host the services to which the metadata refers. A catalog portal that provides map-viewing tools tends to be more generic than other types of portals. Catalog portals are useful when they cater to a wide variety of services and providers because service providers only need to provide metadata in standard format. As a result, SDI often uses these kinds of portals.

A key design consideration in catalog portals is how to build and maintain the catalog. Many portals provide an interface through which service providers create and maintain metadata or allow them to submit metadata in agreed formats. This can be inefficient because service providers must remember to update the portal whenever they modify or create new metadata records. Updating portals can become time consuming for large information suppliers that register services on multiple portals. Some portals, therefore, build automatic routines that access remote metadata databases over the Web. This means that if an organization creates and maintains its own metadata database, the portal can access this and automatically extract new or updated metadata records. The portal does this in one of two ways. In the centralized approach, the catalog portal routinely collects, or harvests, metadata from remote sources

Librarians use similar harvesting techniques to assemble catalogs and have established a number of well-defined international standards. The geospatial industry is adopting some of these standards, in particular Z39.50, Open Archive Initiative (OAI) Metadata Harvesting protocols, as the basis for spatial metadata harvesting.

then consolidates it within a central database at the portal. In the distributed approach, the metadata is kept at the service providers' sites, and the portal queries the sites when it receives a search request from a user. The latter approach has proven difficult to implement, as search speed and reliability entirely depend on the robustness of the network and distributed metadata databases. Therefore, most portals maintain their catalogs using a combination of automatic harvesting and manual updating.

Typical system architecture of a catalog portal consists of a local database management system containing the metadata catalog and local geospatial data used to orient users undertaking spatial metadata searches. The system uses an Internet map server to create maps, undertake spatial queries, and manage metadata and a Web server to organize and present the portal interface on the Web. It is now possible to build catalog portals from a combination of standard off-the-shelf GIS and IT industry Web software.

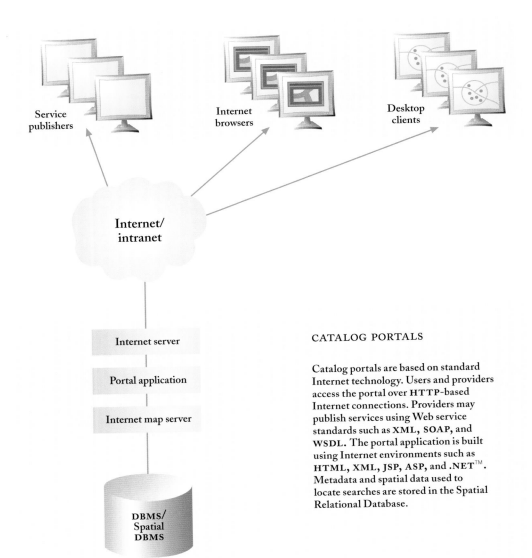

Service
publishers

Internet
browsers

Desktop
clients

Internet/
intranet

Internet server

Portal application

Internet map server

DBMS/
Spatial
DBMS

CATALOG PORTALS

Catalog portals are based on standard
Internet technology. Users and providers
access the portal over HTTP-based
Internet connections. Providers may
publish services using Web service
standards such as XML, SOAP, and
WSDL. The portal application is built
using Internet environments such as
HTML, XML, JSP, ASP, and .NET™.
Metadata and spatial data used to
locate searches are stored in the Spatial
Relational Database.

Application portals combine information services into a Web-based mapping package that generally focuses on a particular task or application. They target well-defined audiences or user requirements and provide efficient access to data and functional services that portal managers select to meet the needs of users. They may or may not include metadata catalogs. Rather than providing generic search tools, application portals provide a structured user interface that guides users to the services they need. An application portal focusing on planning permit submission would, for example, bring together background information, maps, online forms, and specific queries that allow users to check planning regulations that cover the proposed site or the number of public facilities nearby. Often, application portals store some, if not all, of the data and functional services at the portal site.

Application portals generally include dedicated application and data servers that host locally based data and geoprocessing services. Their services are less generic and more complex than catalog servers and may require considerable customization and coordination between service providers. These portals often serve the needs of a particular department or organization rather than being multiparticipant initiatives. They run on local intranets or local area networks (LANs) as well as on the Web.

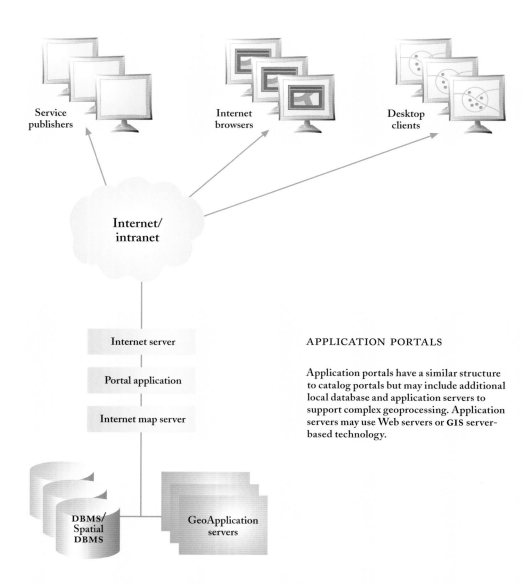

Service
publishers

Internet
browsers

Desktop
clients

Internet/
intranet

Internet server

Portal application

Internet map server

DBMS/
Spatial
DBMS

GeoApplication
servers

APPLICATION PORTALS

Application portals have a similar structure
to catalog portals but may include additional
local database and application servers to
support complex geoprocessing. Application
servers may use Web servers or GIS server-
based technology.

A third type of spatial portal, the enterprise spatial portal, involves the integration of spatial data and functionality with business enterprise solutions. Enterprise solutions appeared in the late 1990s to help large organizations manage distributed information resources. Implemented by companies such as SAP® and Oracle®, they tended to concentrate on office automation, enterprise-wide resource planning, and document handling. They ignored spatial information, at least initially. This is changing as many are now integrating GIS functionality and data into the portal environment. This allows users to switch easily from data in document or spreadsheet form to view related mapped data without having to leave the corporate portal. A utilities enterprise portal could, for example, generate a work order for maintenance at a particular power station and automatically use a spatial function to identify customers affected by the work.

Other organizations do not simply bring spatial resources into the portal but adopt location as the central way to order and search information. This recognizes that a lot of valuable spatial data is often stored in free text format—contract documents, letters, reports, e-mails, spreadsheets, images, and Web pages. Special tools are now available to search and index spatial information from such unstructured documents. Spatial search routines work with electronic document management systems to index references to locations found in documents. Building such indexes allows users to search for all documents that mention a particular location, regardless of type or format. Catalog, application, and enterprise spatial portals have evolved rapidly since the turn of the twenty-first century. This will surely continue as organizations explore the opportunities portals offer and apply them to new fields and new challenges.

CHAPTER 3

Geospatial One-Stop:
Two clicks to content

The Geospatial One-Stop has a simple but powerful aim: to make it easier, faster, and less expensive for all levels of government and the public to access geospatial information. Geospatial One-Stop (GOS) comes with a clear mantra: *Two clicks to content.*

The public referred to above include the more than 281 million people in the United States. Levels of government range from the White House, Congress, and federal agencies to state, tribal, county, and municipal administrations. The content is geospatial information: maps, datasets, images, texts, applications, and models. Hundreds of government, commercial, and noncommercial organizations hold this information on a myriad of Web sites, databases, applications, libraries, and filing cabinets nationwide.

Does GOS face an impossible task? It is certainly a challenge, but the Geospatial One-Stop project is making progress toward its goal. The Office of Management and Budget (OMB) launched GOS in December 2002. Six months later, the team unveiled a prototype spatial portal *(www.geodata. gov)* that delivered on the promise of two clicks to content. Users define their topic of interest with a couple clicks of the mouse. The portal responds with a list of relevant information resources (or services) assembled from databases and directories across the nation. Within a year, users were hitting the site at a rate of about 600 visits per day. By early 2005, more than 500 information providers (or publishers) had registered nearly 100,000 services with the portal, of which more than 1,400 linked directly to live map services. The portal builds real partnerships that have tangible results. It quickly gets data to emergency services, ensuring users can find and access data wherever it is held, reducing search time and duplication, and helping organizations collaborate on new data capture and modeling initiatives. Geospatial One-Stop is attracting worldwide interest as one of the key reference sites for spatial portal development.

What is behind this success? What does the portal actually do, why is it popular, and what lies ahead?

The origins of Geospatial One-Stop

Geospatial One-Stop is part of a wider federal government e-government initiative. The E-Government Act of 2002 made information technology, particularly Internet service delivery, the focus of a drive for more accessible, responsive, and citizen-centered government. The OMB now oversees twenty-four high-profile e-government initiatives designed to improve coordination, access, clarity, and speed of the delivery of information in government-to-citizen, government-to-government, and government-to-business communication. The initiatives target critical areas: disaster management, homeland security, vital statistics, government taxation, and incentive initiatives. One of these projects, Geospatial One-Stop, aims to provide a one-stop source for geospatial information.

Why include geospatial information in this list? Government organizations produce and use vast quantities of geospatial information. Geospatial data plays an integrating role in government, providing resources for homeland security; fighting fires, crime, and disease; attracting investment; repairing roads; managing growth and development; and protecting and preserving the nation's environment and heritage. It makes sense for government organizations with interests in the same location to share and work from the same basic geographic datasets. This avoids duplicated effort, inconsistencies, delays, confusion, and wasted resources.

The earthquake and tsunami that occurred in the Indian Ocean on December 26, 2004, wrought devastation to coastal communities throughout the region. The disaster prompted one of the largest international humanitarian relief operations ever seen. The Office of Management and Budget (OMB) established a dedicated "Indian Ocean Disaster" channel on the Geospatial One-Stop portal to facilitate access to news, information, and spatial data about the affected areas.

Sharing spatial resources was once fraught with difficulty. Users had to contact many organizations to obtain data for any particular area. Because organizations hold their data in different ways, assembling data was often a complex, error-prone, and time-consuming task. Even discovering the existence and location of a particular resource was a challenge, to say nothing of keeping up with an organization's plans to capture or build new resources. An OMB survey uncovered these issues at all government levels. "During the early days of our e-government strategy, we set up focus groups with state and local officials," said Mark Forman, administrator of the Office of Electronic Government and Information Technology at the OMB. "Repeatedly, state and local representatives told us that geospatial information supported their most critical functions. However, we were told that finding and obtaining federal geospatial data was overly burdensome … Users could spend months doing Internet searches, making phone calls, and writing letters to federal agencies in search of geospatial information."

The role of the portal

The Geospatial One-Stop portal gives the GIS community a new way to interact and search for and share resources. The portal reduces search time from months to seconds. Interactive tools let users select an area of interest, define the information needed (by content type, publisher, keyword, or date), and the portal does the rest. It seamlessly searches across regional, administrative, and organizational boundaries. Users enter search criteria once, and the search engine combs the resource inventories of all organizations (government, commercial, or noncommercial) registered with the portal and presents a consolidated list of results matching their criteria. Users have no need to contact individual organizations separately or to repeat the same search on multiple data clearinghouses or inventories. This saves time for the user looking for resources and for the resource providers who must otherwise respond to such queries.

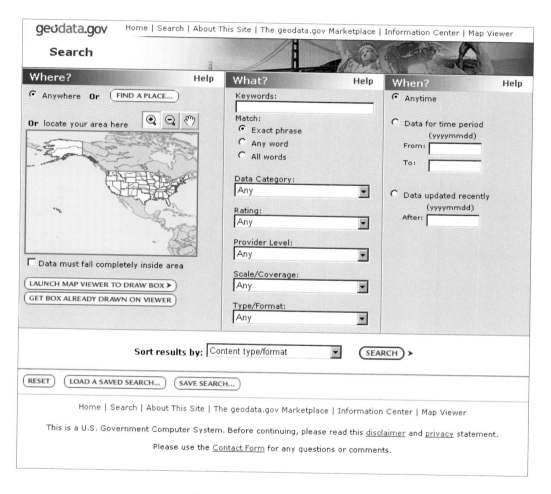

The main search page of the Geospatial One-Stop portal allows users to easily define criteria based on the location, contents, and time covered by an information service.

Putting technology to work

Many other highly innovative Geospatial One-Stop functions feature relatively simple technology while addressing key issues raised by the OMB survey.

For example, users can save search criteria and results, meaning they can refer to or rerun saved searches, making their work much easier. More importantly, they can ask the portal to notify them when it receives new or updated resources that meet their saved criteria. Users are confident they will automatically learn of any relevant change or addition as long as resource holders register with the portal and keep its information current. Users in southern Florida can, for example, receive an alert when a data provider posts new or updated hurricane-related datasets for the area on Geospatial One-Stop. In this way, it is much easier for emergency services, community groups, local authorities, and the public to access consistent, updated data.

Through the portal, users can also share plans for new systems, data-capture initiatives, analyses, models, and other resources. This alerts the user community about resources available in the near future. It brings together users working on similar projects, identifies overlap and duplication, and encourages collaboration and cooperation in spatial resource development.

The portal provides a user-friendly Map Viewer that lets users review and overlay data from completely unrelated sources. This breakthrough in functionality integrates into a single view any combination of Web-mapping services that supports Open Geospatial Consortium (OGC) and other industry-standard specifications. The viewer handles reprojections necessary to bring data from different projections into a single map window and allows users to set transparency level and the order of map layers. It also displays the legends and related information from multiple data sources. Users can print maps or save them as Internet links with the "Save Map Link" option to share them with others online.

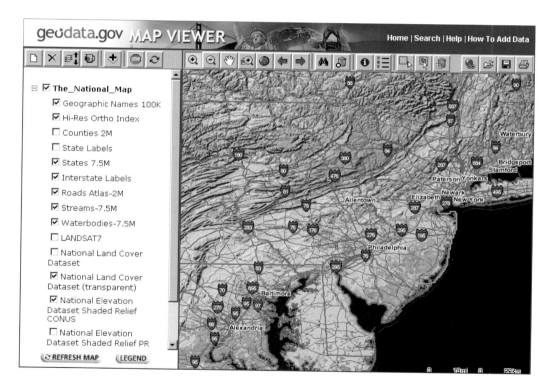

The Geospatial One-Stop Map Viewer provides a user-friendly environment that lets users view and navigate live datasets discovered through the portal. They can integrate data services coming from different remote sources, add data from their local networks, interrogate and query the data, and print and save their maps.

Users also can access data through seventeen data categories or channels. These channels can be thought of as shortcuts to preselected featured data. The channels group primary information resources into broad geographical themes covering such areas as transport networks, biology and ecology, cadastral theme, imagery, and basemaps. A team of specialists with expertise in the channel's subject matter manages and organizes channel content. Experts come from many different organizations throughout the country. This ensures updated and relevant channel content. It also encourages participation in managing and sharing spatial resources and stimulates communication and cooperation between organizations. The channel stewards also have responsibility for seeking input from others in the field to strengthen participation as they develop the channel.

The government's GOS team can create temporary channels in response to a particular event or situation, such as a security alert, sporting event, or natural disaster demanding rapid pooling of information resources. For example, the team created dedicated channels for a number of the large hurricanes that hit the East Coast of the United States in 2003 and 2004. The channels assembled topographic, land ownership, shelter, and emergency facility map resources throughout the affected areas. Detailed local and regional weather services provided forecast and near real-time weather reports, precipitation counts, and water levels in the region's rivers and tidal stations. Federal, state, local, and commercial data providers participated. Many had already published data through Geospatial One-Stop; others made their data available in response to the emergency. Such dedicated channels made it easier and faster for emergency services, local officials, and the public to access and coordinate essential datasets. Once again, the project strived toward the goal of "two clicks to content."

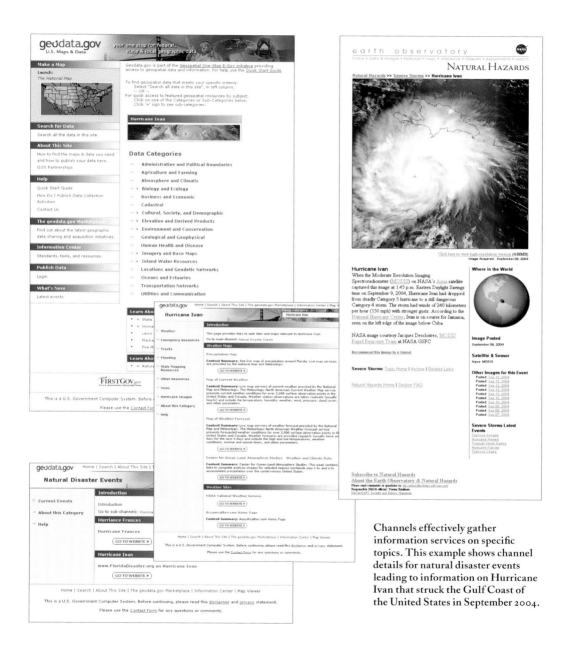

Channels effectively gather
information services on specific
topics. This example shows channel
details for natural disaster events
leading to information on Hurricane
Ivan that struck the Gulf Coast of
the United States in September 2004.

Developing Geospatial One-Stop

The OMB enlisted the help of ESRI in Redlands, California, to establish the portal. ESRI had gained practical experience from a number of high-profile portal initiatives, including the pioneering Geography Network. The company also had worked with other government and nongovernment organizations on major Web map projects such as the National Geographic's MapEngine and the Bureau of Land Management's NILS portal. The Geospatial One-Stop portal uses ArcSDE® 9.0 to manage database transactions and ArcIMS® 9.0 for Internet mapping services. An ArcIMS Metadata Service allows data providers to submit metadata or create it online through specially designed Web interfaces. The service also allows GOS managers to review and manage metadata records and provides search and discovery tools for users. Web, application, and data servers run on multiple machines to support around-the-clock operation and high demand.

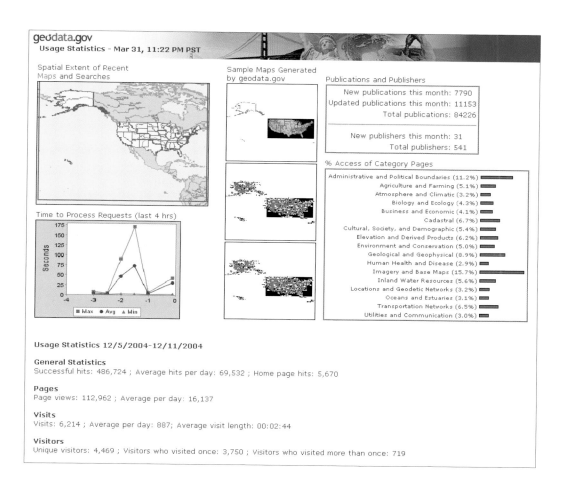

geodata.gov
Usage Statistics - Mar 31, 11:22 PM PST

Spatial Extent of Recent
Maps and Searches

Time to Process Requests (last 4 hrs)

Seconds: 175 150 125 100 75 50 25 0

-4 -3 -2 -1 0

■ Max ● Avg ▲ Min

Sample Maps Generated
by geodata.gov

Publications and Publishers

New publications this month: 7790
Updated publications this month: 11153
Total publications: 84226

New publishers this month: 31
Total publishers: 541

% Access of Category Pages

Administrative and Political Boundaries (11.2%)
Agriculture and Farming (5.1%)
Atmosphere and Climatic (3.2%)
Biology and Ecology (4.3%)
Business and Economic (4.1%)
Cadastral (6.7%)
Cultural, Society, and Demographic (5.4%)
Elevation and Derived Products (6.2%)
Environment and Conservation (5.0%)
Geological and Geophysical (8.9%)
Human Health and Disease (2.9%)
Imagery and Base Maps (15.7%)
Inland Water Resources (5.6%)
Locations and Geodetic Networks (3.2%)
Oceans and Estuaries (3.1%)
Transportation Networks (6.5%)
Utilities and Communication (3.0%)

Usage Statistics 12/5/2004-12/11/2004

General Statistics
Successful hits: 486,724 ; Average hits per day: 69,532 ; Home page hits: 5,670

Pages
Page views: 112,962 ; Average per day: 16,137

Visits
Visits: 6,214 ; Average per day: 887; Average visit length: 00:02:44

Visitors
Unique visitors: 4,469 ; Visitors who visited once: 3,750 ; Visitors who visited more than once: 719

Geospatial One-Stop managers can track the volume and nature of site usage through detailed statistics pages. This includes tracking the number of services, additions, updates, and user access statistics. The red bars on the right break down user access by category of information, which indicates the most popular types of information in the past month. Maps display the extent of recent user searches, while the graph at bottom shows the maximum, minimum, and average speed of searches in the last four hours.

Expanding and keeping Geospatial One-Stop current requires consistent effort. This includes encouraging new partners to register their resources and helping existing partners to maintain and update resources registered previously. The work involves constantly reviewing and enhancing functionality and exploring new ways to build and share data and applications. In January 2005, for example, OMB commissioned the second release of Geospatial One-Stop that pioneers the combination of the Google text search engine with spatial search functions. This brings unprecedented speed and flexibility to metadata searches. The enhancements in this version also concentrate on improving the way users and managers work with the portal, making it easier for them to create and save their own environment. Users can personalize their own portal pages, making it even easier to access the services they need and to organize online workgroups and collaborations. A more sophisticated metadata management system gives service providers greater control over who can view or access metadata registered with the portal. Providers can share material with selected groups of users, enabling Geospatial One-Stop to provide a secure environment to disseminate sensitive services (for example, work-in-progress or proprietary or classified information).

Work is needed to align how organizations view or model real-world features. The portal allows users to share and exchange data easily, but data integration will remain complex unless organizations working within a similar field agree on common data models. The GOS team is building consensus among user organizations on generic models for key (or framework) data-sets and how to organize (and fund) their transition.

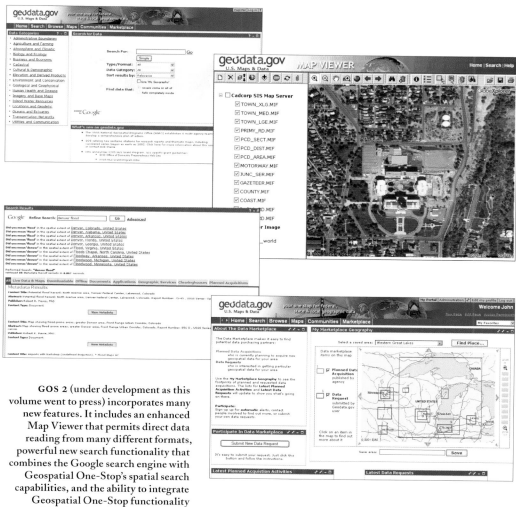

GOS 2 (under development as this volume went to press) incorporates many new features. It includes an enhanced Map Viewer that permits direct data reading from many different formats, powerful new search functionality that combines the Google search engine with Geospatial One-Stop's spatial search capabilities, and the ability to integrate Geospatial One-Stop functionality with other portals. This opens new opportunities for users to harness the power of Geospatial One-Stop to build new, personalized portals.

Lessons learned and looking ahead

Three principles have guided the development of the portal so far, offering hope for the future.

First, the team has built a collaborative environment. Though the project is a federal government initiative, any organization, including government, academic, nonprofit, or commercial, holding data relevant to the United States can publish data through Geospatial One-Stop.

Online communities are developing by sharing resources, plans, and initiatives such as the channel steward program. Similarly, Geospatial One-Stop aims to be inclusive: anyone with an Internet connection can access the portal and use information found through it. The Geospatial One-Stop portal also works with screen readers and voice-activated computers. It fully complies with Section 508 of the Rehabilitation Act, which supports access by people with disabilities to federal electronic and information technology.

The portal functionality also encourages participation. Consider, for example, the submission and maintenance of metadata, potentially one of the most time-consuming tasks for data publishers. Publishers can submit metadata in two commonly used, independent standards (FGDC and ISO). Since many organizations already maintain their own metadata clearinghouse repositories, Geospatial One-Stop permits the automatic harvesting of metadata. This eliminates duplication and leverages past investments. Automatic harvesting also provides choice as the harvesting routines support standards from the library (Z39.50 and the Open Archive Initiative), GIS (ArcIMS Metadata Server), and general IT (Web-accessible folder) worlds. In addition, service providers can enter or update metadata directly through online forms or upload records in ASCII text, eXtensible Markup Language (XML), and Standard Generalized Markup Language (SGML). Geospatial One-Stop attempts, wherever possible, to provide choice and options that encourage inclusion.

Second, the portal and the project as a whole has taken a practical and feasible approach, using available resources to deliver tangible benefits. Existing COTS software and tested techniques form the basis of the current portal. Taking the example of metadata again, the portal administrators run an automatic verification procedure on every metadata record before loading it into the system. This may seem overly cautious, but experience shows that organizations may interpret the standard differently. They may use varied approaches to metadata accuracy and currency, even when they use the same standard. Metadata catalogs can degrade very quickly without such simple checks.

The emphasis on the practical not only begins to tackle problems of efficiency, duplication, and so on but also provides a concrete, working demonstration of the long-term vision of realizing a National Spatial Data Infrastructure. The Geospatial One-Stop portal is the first step toward this goal, motivating participation, dialog, and greater understanding of the remaining objectives and hurdles.

Finally, Geospatial One-Stop has built on the work of other projects and initiatives. This includes the long-running and influential work of the Federal Geographic Data Committee (FGDC) which is responsible for defining and promoting NSDI and standards for geospatial metadata. A number of federal agencies have independently been addressing issues relevant to Geospatial One-Stop. They have tried to bring data models into harmony and simplify access and maintenance. Such projects, like the U.S. Geological Survey's *The National Map*, offer valuable experience and the basis for generic framework datasets. Geospatial One-Stop lends support to and builds on these programs.

The Geospatial One-Stop portal makes it possible to search and assemble data and services in a fraction of the time it took before. It also supports new communities and collaborations that work together to develop new resources, including data, data structures, and applications. For service suppliers and users, Geospatial One-Stop improves productivity and the return on investments in geospatial data and resources and builds a framework for an efficient, open, robust NSDI.

CHAPTER 4

GeoNorge:
A national map portal
for Norway

National governments perform a delicate balancing act to provide security, health, education, and opportunity for their citizens. Needs, interests, expectations, and solutions often vary greatly from one place to the next. Programs that work in an urban, industrial setting are often unfeasible, expensive, or simply irrelevant to rural farming communities, and vice versa.

This applies to national mapping programs too. Good planning and government require accurate, up-to-date maps, regardless of the area covered. But can governments with finite resources (hardware, software, manpower, and skills) justify detailed mapping of small communities and sparsely populated areas? How regularly should governments update their maps and at what scale? How can national governments ensure that local communities have access to available data? Ultimately, who pays?

These issues are relevant in most countries, but nowhere more so than in Norway, a country renowned worldwide for the quality and consistency of its welfare and public services. Yet Norway offers a stark contrast between its urban heartland and surrounding rural countryside. Of Norway's total population, 11 percent live in Oslo, the nation's capital, and 45 percent reside in provinces falling within 100 kilometers (63 miles) of the city. With few exceptions, settlements are small and dispersed outside the urban centers of the southeast. The nation's 434 municipalities range in size from 6 square kilometers (2.32 square miles) to 9,700 square kilometers (3,745 square miles) and in population from 200 to 500,000. Resources available for mapmaking also vary.

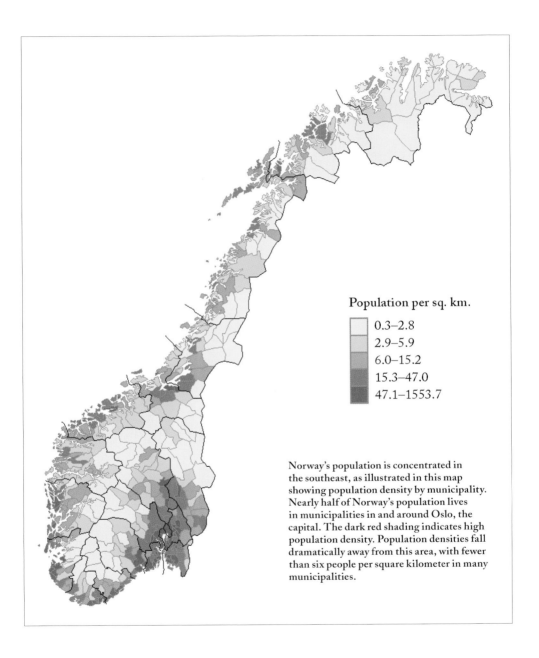

Population per sq. km.

- 0.3–2.8
- 2.9–5.9
- 6.0–15.2
- 15.3–47.0
- 47.1–1553.7

Norway's population is concentrated in the southeast, as illustrated in this map showing population density by municipality. Nearly half of Norway's population lives in municipalities in and around Oslo, the capital. The dark red shading indicates high population density. Population densities fall dramatically away from this area, with fewer than six people per square kilometer in many municipalities.

Norway has addressed the problem of mapping remote regions by building partnerships between public agencies and private industry. For years, Statens Kartverk, the Norwegian Mapping Authority (NMA), has fostered collaborative mapping initiatives between local and regional governments, national agencies, and private businesses. These organizations share an interest in producing and maintaining good, up-to-date maps. In 2003, the Norwegian government reviewed these programs and endorsed a plan, Norway Digital, to strengthen and broaden their impact and develop a national spatial data infrastructure. Spatial portals lie at the heart of this plan.

Working together

Norway Digital cuts horizontally across boundaries between national government agencies and vertically through all levels of government. While focusing on government agencies, the plan embraces the private and public sectors and involves the creation of a national geospatial framework made up of multiple spatial portals serving different communities and needs. Portals will host standards-based data and functionality that participating members can use to build their own sites and services. Central to the plan is geoNorge *(www.geoNorge.no)*, a new NMA portal that hosts key topographic map services and provides indexing and search functionality across the entire framework.

Norway Digital builds on significant collaborative mapping programs, including the Geovekst program originating in 1992. NMA previously mapped at scales up to 1:50,000 while local authorities mapped their areas at more detailed scales. For many smaller local authorities, this was a considerable challenge. The Geovekst, or "geo-growth" program, helps coordinate and fund large-scale national mapping. Founding members included the NMA; state road, agriculture, and telecommunications departments; regional and municipal governments; and a group of electricity companies. Railway, telecommunication, and other organizations joined later.

Norway Digital envisions a loosely coupled network of portals organized into three layers. At the base are local or regional portals providing information on specific areas or issues. Municipalities, local communities, private organizations, and focused research groups within national agencies will develop and maintain such portals. National government agency portals form the next tier. These organizations maintain portals serving national datasets as well as linking to relevant regional or local portals. The geoNorge portal forms the last tier and provides central indexing and search capability. It provides a one-stop shop for spatial searches, allowing users to search for resources on any of the other portals in the Norway Digital network.

While coordinated by NMA, Geovekst participants collectively identify priorities, create mapping programs, develop data requirements and specifications, and issue contracts. Independent mapping companies compete for these contracts and work under the supervision of Geovekst members. Participants share costs based on their ability to pay and their interest in the particular dataset in question. Contributors have equal rights to the data produced, regardless of the amount each pays, and can use it freely. Organizations outside the Geovekst partnership can use the data but must pay for it. The income finances operational costs and future data capture programs. Geovekst helps to ensure that large-scale maps are consistent throughout the nation and that smaller, rural municipalities have up-to-date maps of their lands.

Other initiatives address thematic issues or datasets. The Arealis program coordinated by NMA and the Ministry of Environment promotes development of land use and environmental spatial datasets in national, regional, and local governments. Participation includes more than twenty agencies in ten national government departments plus local authorities and many municipalities. Arealis has developed a consolidated database holding 150 layers of environmental and land-use information that now extends across large parts of Norway.

These programs have helped develop and maintain high-quality spatial datasets throughout Norway. Yet many local municipalities and counties still lack the resources to use or access the datasets. This includes the necessary hardware, software, and skills to manage datasets locally and the required resources to build and maintain functionality. The continued success of Geovekst and Arealis and other initiatives depends on making their benefits available to all participants.

The Arealis interface brings together many datasets relating to environmental management and land-use planning. Data comes from different agencies, research groups, and municipalities. Arealis allows users to view and interrogate this data within a single system interface, minimizing time spent searching for and obtaining data.

GeoNorge and the portal framework

Norway Digital and the portal framework offer a solution by encouraging participants to host data and services through Web portals. Individual participants will develop and maintain portals that conform to agreed standards. The central geoNorge portal maintains an index of available services, making it easier for users to search and identify relevant spatial information and functionality. National agencies such as NMA can ensure access to Geovekst and Arealis datasets through robust, centrally hosted services. The portal allows users to search for data based on location, keyword, scale, source organization, or date of production. It also provides a comprehensive Internet mapping application that allows users to select, integrate, and view data from many different portals within the Norway Digital framework. Thus, for example, it is possible to bring in and view administrative boundaries from NMA's servers with land-use classifications from the Arealis dataset and subsurface geology from the Geological Survey of Norway. The geoNorge portal also provides generic templates for mapping services and commonly used functions like printing, analysis, and search which will help municipalities set up their own dedicated spatial portals.

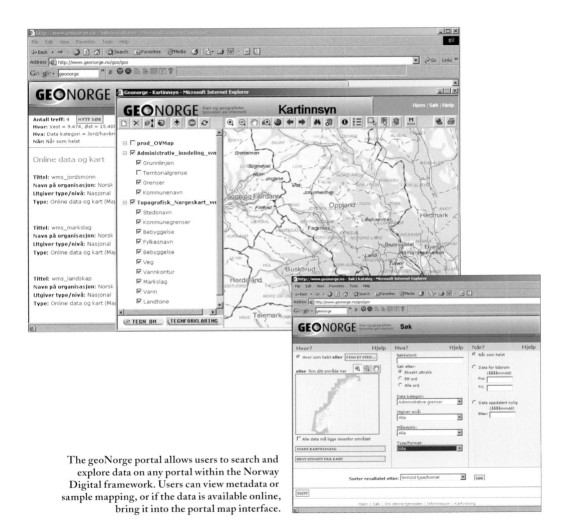

The geoNorge portal allows users to search and explore data on any portal within the Norway Digital framework. Users can view metadata or sample mapping, or if the data is available online, bring it into the portal map interface.

The portal framework has expanded quickly. Many key portals are already up and running, particularly within national agencies. Rapid agreement on standards helped speed this process. Through Geovekst and other collaborative initiatives, many agencies had already adopted common standards for feature classification and data transfer. These projects made organizations aware of the benefits offered by agreed standards and the work and compromises involved in developing and implementing them. Participants in geoNorge quickly reached agreement to use general IT industry standards such as eXtensible Markup Language (XML), Simple Object Access Protocol (SOAP), and Universal Description, Discovery, and Integration (UDDI) for defining and cataloging services. They also agreed to use OGC's Web Map Service (WMS) and Web Feature Service (WFS) protocols for defining Web map services.

One of the major reasons for Norway Digital's success is the well-established Systematic Organization of Spatial Information (SOSI) standard. This defines feature class and transfer protocols for spatial data in 44 application domains including property, road, utilities, administration, planning, and so on. Working groups made up of organizations using spatial dataset and maintain these standards. Membership of these groups is voluntary and open to all, and they produce standards based on consensus. Though NMA provides organizational assistance and ensures standards are in line with international practice, it does not greatly influence the work of these groups. With a long history (development started in 1977) and a proven structure in which to explore and agree on standards, SOSI greatly facilitated the development and adoption of Norway Digital.

Collaboration may have limited the adoption of well-defined metadata throughout Norway. Many organizations participated in Geovekst and other programs and helped formulate data specifications and contract documents. They were therefore very familiar with the datasets these initiatives produced and, as a result, perhaps had less incentive to develop formal structured metadata.

The creation of metadata is now a priority for Norway Digital. NMA and other agencies defined a series of metadata profiles covering thematic vector data, imagery, and raster datasets. These are compatible with and build on the ISO19115 standard. As full compliance with ISO19115 is a significant undertaking (requiring completion of some 450 elements), the Norwegian Metadata profile identifies a subset of mandatory elements (125 for the thematic vector standard). NMA is also working on developing standard interpretation, keyword, and thesaurus references for consistent data entry and search definition.

The initial version of the central geoNorge portal debuted in February 2004. NMA adopted the ESRI ArcIMS Portal Toolkit as the basis of portal development. Development is based on a collection of commercial off-the-shelf Internet software and uses ArcIMS 4.01 for Internet mapping and ArcSDE 8.3 and Oracle® 9.2 for database management. This provided a robust, tested application that met international and Open Geospatial Consortium (OGC) standards. The Portal Toolkit supported rapid development and deployment and allowed NMA to launch the initial version of the portal within six weeks of project commencement. Users of the prototype provided valuable feedback that NMA incorporated in the final release launched in November 2004.

Looking to the future

Norway Digital has achieved much since its launch. The geoNorge portal provides a gateway to a growing network of portals. Standards permit exchange and reuse of data and services, and more organizations are publishing detailed metadata describing the services they offer. Regional and local participants have greater access to spatial data and functionality.

Challenges remain. Only a small number of local municipalities have established their own portals. Creating localized portals would allow them to organize the data and tools that geoNorge offers to target local concerns more effectively. Initiatives are now exploring how to provide technology and skills to support such local portals. Organizations are providing metadata for their datasets, but few have experience in the arduous task of long-term maintenance and auditing of metadata records.

Other countries could benefit from Norway's approach to consistent national mapping. The Geovekst and Arealis stories show how national, regional, and local governments can work with private organizations to build comprehensive nationwide datasets. The geoNorge portal and the portal framework defined by Norway Digital make these resources available to all, no matter where they live.

CHAPTER 5

Transport Direct:
Keeping Britain
on the move

Navigating public transportation can be a challenge, particularly in an unfamiliar place. Travelers inevitably end up struggling with a fistful of maps and leaflets describing the routes, schedules, and fares of different transportation operators. Visitors are left stitching together a combination of services that take them along the quickest, cheapest, or perhaps most scenic route. Travel call centers and Web sites help, but often they concentrate on services of a single operator, type of transportation, city, or region. If the journey requires a combination of services or extends beyond city or regional boundaries, planning can become time consuming and frustrating. The British Government's Department for Transport (DfT) leads a team that recently launched Transport Direct, a spatial portal that links independent information services to offer a one-stop shop for travel information nationwide.

Transport Direct allows travelers to view travel options, plan journeys, compare costs, buy tickets, predict journey times, and even keep up with real-time traffic conditions. When complete, Transport Direct will cover all modes of travel—air, car, train, tram, subway, taxi, bus, ferry, bicycle, and even foot—and allow users to plan journeys using any combination. DfT released an Internet version of the service in July 2004 and intends to expand this to allow users access to the portal through a nationwide network of kiosks and mobile phones, personal digital assistants (PDAs), and eventually, digital televisions.

The Transport Direct portal allows people to plan journeys from one end of the United Kingdom to the other, combining all modes of transport from the rural bus or ferry to city subway systems.

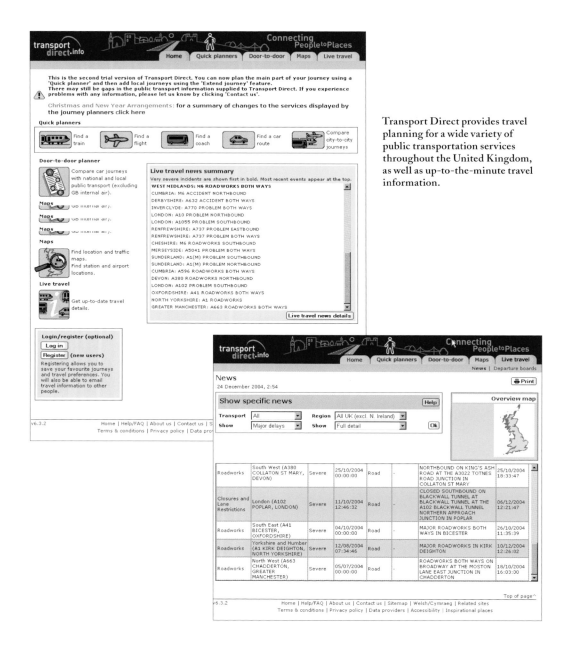

Transport Direct provides travel planning for a wide variety of public transportation services throughout the United Kingdom, as well as up-to-the-minute travel information.

Motivation for implementing the new portal goes beyond helping frustrated visitors, however. DfT's research suggests that the general public is often unaware of available public transportation services. The report found this resulted from the public's overwhelming reliance on the private car and the difficulty in finding information about public transportation. Service operators, transportation groups, and local governments provide plenty of information, but it is highly dispersed and uncoordinated, making it difficult for the public to find and use. For the government in the United Kingdom, as in many other countries, building a successful public transportation system is key to addressing problems such as road congestion and air pollution and fostering more sustainable, environmentally friendly travel. Ensuring that the public is aware of its travel options is an essential part of this strategy.

The challenge

In January 2003, DfT appointed an interdisciplinary consortium lead by Atos Origin to design, develop, and run Transport Direct. The team faced an unprecedented challenge. No one had attempted to build a national integrated travel information service for a country with a transportation system as complex or dense as that in the United Kingdom. Hundreds of organizations provide transportation information, including private transportation operators, regional and municipal authorities, police, highway authorities, and consumer and industry groups. There are millions of services, route maps, timetables, connections and fare rates, and numerous ways to combine services for a single journey. Data is dynamic. Traffic conditions change by the minute because of accidents, maintenance work, the weather, rail closures, revised timetables and services, and so on. Though national in coverage, the system will be judged on the accuracy of local information. Maintaining up-to-the-minute information on the national rail network, for example, is useless if information about the local bus or taxi connections at the destination is wrong.

Implementing Transport Direct requires a range of skills and expertise. The European IT services company, Atos Origin, assembled a consortium that includes some of the leading companies in the field. Atos Origin undertakes overall project management and oversees design, construction, and maintenance of the portal. Microsoft® supports the implementation of its .NET technology, while ESRI UK provides mapping software and solutions. The engineering consultants, Atkins, have implemented the coordinated trip-planning solution. BBC Technology and Real Time Engineering Ltd. (RTEL) are developing the user interface and wireless communication network. The project team has more than one hundred members.

Building collaboration

The Transport Direct team could not collect and maintain this vast quantity of data independently. The team decided to create an application portal to work with existing travel information services rather than attempt to replace or duplicate them. With this approach, users enter details about their proposed journey into the portal. The portal analyzes the travel details, retrieves information from relevant information providers, and consolidates and presents the results. From a single location, the public can obtain travel information from and to anywhere in the country. The portal also ensures clear, independent information on all viable transportation options for a proposed route. Travelers now can make informed choices about which services to use based on cost, travel time, convenience, or other considerations.

This approach depended entirely on collaboration with existing information suppliers. Early on, the team spent a lot of time building an open, inclusive environment. This was no easy task in the United Kingdom's intensely competitive transportation industry. The team used workshops and forums for local authorities, transportation operators, and trade associations to explain project goals, present initial designs and pilot studies, and gather feedback. An advisory board includes representatives from industry, transportation groups, and local government. The board reviews and advises on strategic, technical, and marketing decisions taken by the project team. Initially, this helped engage organizations in the project, allowing them to raise concerns and participate in business decisions.

By the time the system went live in July 2004, more than 140 transportation organizations were participating in Transport Direct, and over 200 companies were supplying data.

Travel planning with Transport Direct

The portal homepage, found at *www.transportdirect.info,* presents a summary of live travel news as well as options to plan journeys by air, bus, rail, car, or any combination.

Travel news provides details of accidents, delays, and maintenance work on the road and rail networks and at the country's ports and airports. An external data partner assembles news items from over 100 different sources and updates Transport Direct every fifteen minutes. Information includes location, type of incident, severity, date and time of occurrence, and the operators involved.

Planning a journey with Transport Direct is a simple three-step process. Users select the mode of travel; enter details about the journey, including start and destination and the dates and times of the outward, and if necessary, return trips; and the portal returns information on details of routes and services available. Users can complete a query in minutes.

The system allows users to identify the nearest public transportation facility to their current location. A comprehensive gazetteer (geographical dictionary) of UK place names helps users easily identify locations.

The portal presents summary information for all feasible options, including the number of changes required, start and end times, and total duration. Selecting a particular option allows users to explore additional information, including the exact route and timing of each leg of the journey. They can view detailed mapping showing the proposed route and points of interest such as tourist or administrative sites, hotels, taxi ranks, and so on. Alternatively, they can display route information as easy-to-read schematic graphics or step-by-step written directions. If a journey requires a walk between segments (for example, transferring from a bus station to the subway), the portal calculates walking route and the time involved. For journeys by car or bus, the portal shows predicted traffic densities along the route and incorporates this information in estimates of speed and journey duration. Traffic density information is based on years of congestion surveys and traffic analyses and varies depending on the time, day of the week, season, and so on. The user can set and save certain preferences, such as walking and driving speed, which the application takes into account when calculating journey times.

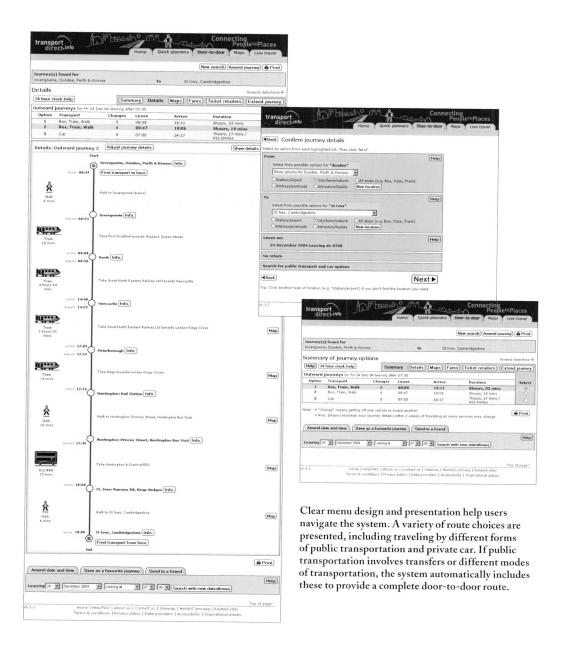

Clear menu design and presentation help users navigate the system. A variety of route choices are presented, including traveling by different forms of public transportation and private car. If public transportation involves transfers or different modes of transportation, the system automatically includes these to provide a complete door-to-door route.

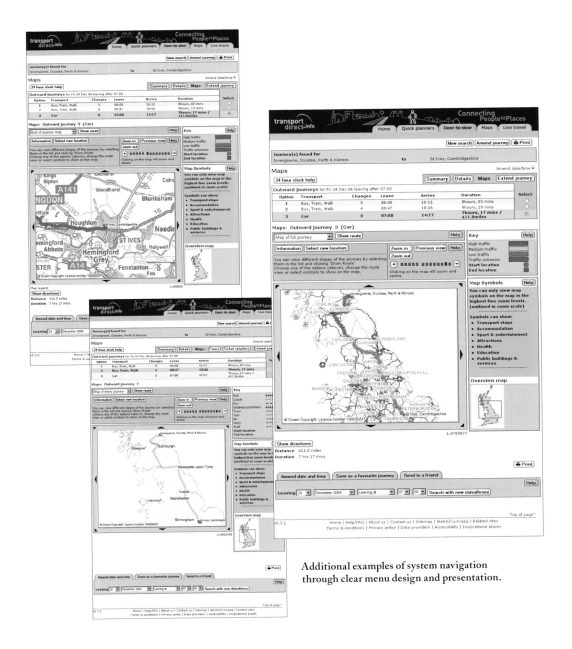

Additional examples of system navigation through clear menu design and presentation.

Users can also check whether trains are running on schedule. The portal can display arrival and departure information for any station in the country, highlighting delayed or cancelled trains. Someone meeting a passenger can check the latest anticipated arrival times before leaving for the station. Similar functionality is available for certain bus services.

Once users decide on a particular service, the portal directs them to Web sites where they book and pay for tickets. Options also allow users to extend trips so that, for example, they can use the flight planner to search for a suitable flight and then extend the journey to discover travel options from the airport to the final destination. Users can print or save journey plans for later referral or e-mail them to friends or colleagues.

Building the portal

The portal holds a collection of Web, GIS, journey planning, and database servers. The Web servers handle presentation and communication with the end user and link to external sites that provide real-time travel updates for road and rail services, and for booking and ticket sales.

Fourteen GIS servers handle location queries and generate maps. Travel-planning sessions begin with users identifying the starts and destinations of their journeys. The system contains a comprehensive gazetteer, or geographical dictionary, containing some 30 million addresses, 300,000 bus stops, 2,500 train stations, 72 airports, and many other transport locations throughout the country. It also stores the location of tourist attractions, sports centers, government offices, and other facilities. GIS servers match locations entered by the user to records in the gazetteer to ensure that spelling is correct and that the location is correctly identified before passing information on to the journey planners. Functions allow users to check their positions with reference to detailed mapping and to search for the nearest stations, bus stops, airports, or other transportation modes. Once journey planning systems return a route, the GIS servers will generate and present the related maps, graphics, or driving instructions. These show the proposed routes, traffic conditions, and local information. ArcSDE manages the gazetteer and all other map and geographic information. ArcIMS provides map display and navigation tools.

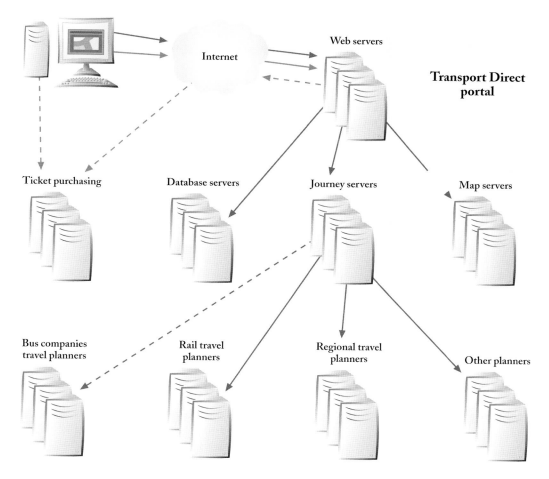

Web servers

Internet

Transport Direct portal

Ticket purchasing

Database servers

Journey servers

Map servers

Bus companies travel planners

Rail travel planners

Regional travel planners

Other planners

The Transport Direct portal links information services to provide a one-stop shop for travel information in the United Kingdom.

Once the GIS servers confirm details of the proposed journey, the portal passes this information to one of six internal Journey Planning servers. These servers handle car routing and run the Coordinated Journey Planner that communicates with external information services. In 2004 when the system was launched, Transport Direct used fourteen different external journey-planning systems. These included nine regional Traveline partnerships run by local authorities and transportation operators that provide bus, tram, light rail, and ferry information; the Association of Train Operating Companies (ATOC) that provides information on the national rail network; individual bus companies which provide information on their own long distance services; and a number of other information services providing data on air travel and local taxis. The Coordinated Journey Planner analyzes the proposed route and establishes which external information services hold relevant information. It passes details about the proposed trip to these services and receives and consolidates the information returned. Consolidation may involve combining information from several services, particularly, for example, if the journey is long and uses a number of different types of transportation. To ensure smooth transitions without gaps between journey legs, the Coordinated Journey Planner must take arrival times generated by one service and pass them to the next. This complex process may take several iterations to resolve.

The database servers store user preferences, administration data, and the gazetteer and map database.

The portal depends on efficient communication between many different systems. Organizations operate these systems, often using different hardware, software, applications, and data formats. The project team used a practical approach to establish communication standards and protocols between these. The team adopted existing IT or transportation industry standards when they were effective and widely supported. However, the team amended the standards when necessary to achieve the high levels of integration and performance required by Transport Direct. The project developed a number of new eXtensible Markup Language-based (XML) standards to describe access and exit points from stations and stops in the public transportation network, for electronic timetable schedules, and for communication between journey-planning software.

The road ahead

The design and the approach to building and maintaining the collaborative environment on which Transport Direct depends is attracting interest from other countries thinking about establishing similar systems. The number of users is rising steeply, and DfT set a target of ten million user sessions per year by the end of 2006. The portal is developing as additional operators and services join, and expansion plans include services in both Northern Ireland and the Republic of Ireland. Plans envision working with commercial companies to offer premium services that may, for example, offer dedicated travel information about specific routes or services and personalized services that automatically inform users of events that may affect their travel.

Transport Direct has delivered on the promise of one-stop travel planning for the United Kingdom. The portal brings together information and offers simple, easy-to-use travel planning for the British public and foreign visitors. It is too early to evaluate Transport Direct's full impact, but cleaner city air and less-congested roads will result if even a fraction of the anticipated users leave their cars at home in favor of public transportation.

CHAPTER 6

MAPSTER:
Managing the waters
of the Canadian Pacific

You are never far from water in Canada's Pacific region, with its 27,000 kilometers (16,777 miles) of rugged coastline, 105 major river systems, and countless smaller rivers, streams, and freshwater lakes. These waters host a rich and diverse marine and aquatic ecology. They serve as the thoroughfares and breeding grounds for salmon and sea trout, some of the most important migratory fish in the North Pacific. Water also plays a critical role in the economic activities of the region, including the timber, hydroelectric, pulp and paper, and tourism industries on which many people depend.

Protecting Canada's waters

Fisheries and Oceans Canada (DFO) is the federal department responsible for safeguarding national economic, ecological, and scientific interests in Canada's oceans and inland waters. The department works to develop and promote safe, effective, and environmentally sound policy and management programs and to conserve and ensure sustainable use of Canada's fisheries.

Creating and implementing good policy depends on effective collection, management, analysis, and most importantly, sharing of data. This involves ensuring that data flows effectively through the department's network of offices, field stations, laboratories, and research centers. It also means sharing data with the department's many stakeholders—the provincial, territorial, and local governments; First Nations; industry and community groups; schools; and academic research institutes. Improving access to information is a key step in fulfilling the department's wider responsibilities and goals. The Oceans, Habitat, and Enhancement Branch (OHEB) of DFO's Pacific Regional office recently launched a new portal site to do just that.

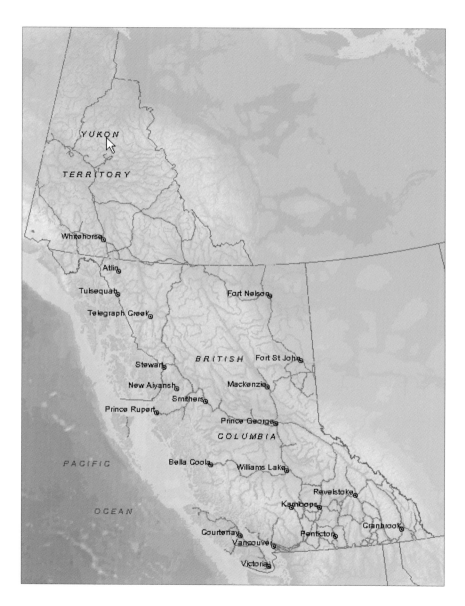

DFO's Pacific Region covers British Columbia and the Yukon Territory and includes some 27,000 kilometers (16,777 miles) of coastline and over one hundred major river systems.

One of OHEB's projects is the Robertson Creek Hatchery *(www–heb.pac.dfo–mpo.gc.ca/ facilities/robertson/background_e.htm)*. The hatchery contributes significantly to commercial fisheries and supports major recreational and First Nations fisheries from Alaska to the west coast of Vancouver Island. The hatchery also supports education and fish culture in community programs and First Nations facilities in Barkley Sound by providing eggs and juvenile fry and through technical support. Fifteen thousand people visit the hatchery annually and take self-directed tours. An additional 5,000 people participate in interactive hatchery programs there.

The OHEB establishes and monitors habitat inventories and conserves and protects fish and fish habitat. Through extensive fieldwork, the agency develops and implements specific measures to enhance or restore fish stocks. Its work depends on close cooperation with local communities. Community education and involvement are important. Staff routinely use a wide range of information, including topographic, hydrographic, social, and economic datasets; biological data; tidal, flow, and temperature readings; fish population surveys; local development plans and proposals; regulatory information; and resource activities and users. Data comes in many formats. It originates from within the department, regular or one-off surveys, other federal departments, industry and third party research, and community groups.

Locating, accessing, and integrating these datasets often proved challenging and extremely time consuming to OHEB staff. A 2003 survey on the effectiveness of data handling in OHEB showed the need for a system to help staff find and use important data. To meet that need, OHEB developed MAPSTER 2.0, a highly structured spatial portal that provides quick and easy access to key spatial datasets and functionality.

Portal requirements

Representatives from various geographic and business areas of OHEB created an Information Management Working Group to guide portal development. The group helped identify specific objectives and data requirements. The portal would need to do more than simply serve data because many potential users either had limited access to GIS facilities or had limited familiarity with GIS. For those reasons, the portal also needed basic visualization, editing, upload, and printing capabilities. The Working Group set system requirements for the portal to

- provide remote access to OHEB's own spatial and tabular data resources, including topographic, asset, biological, administrative, and social data;

- access, integrate, and display spatial data held in other organizations;

- provide tools to create and display geographic data, such as delineation of habitat compensation sites or development of referral sites;

- allow users to load and work with their own data (including GPS, CAD, and GIS datasets) within the portal environment; and

- implement a spatial search engine to help staff find relevant services.

Organizing data

The portal launched by OHEB's GIS Unit in March 2004 provides direct access to more than 200 datasets covering the region. Most datasets came from OHEB's Spatial Data Warehouse, a spatial data server managed by the OHEB GIS Unit based in Vancouver, British Columbia.

Other datasets come from external organizations. The Working Group decided that, wherever possible, users would access this data from the provider's site rather than duplicate it within OHEB. To do this, the development team designed MAPSTER to meet Open Geospatial Consortium (OGC) Web-mapping protocols so that it could use OGC compliant data services hosted by other organizations. For example, the portal provides access to 7,000 Terrain Resource Information Management (TRIM) maps, forest cover classification maps, and hundreds of digital orthophotos covering British Columbia from a Web Map Service (WMS) hosted by the provincial government in Victoria, B.C. The portal also integrates RadarSat™ satellite imagery from the Centre for Remote Sensing in Ottawa, Ontario, accurate urban road network data for emergency 911 response served by a commercial provider in North Vancouver, and small-scale topography and bathymetric layers from as far away as the Netherlands. All are derived from WMS servers.

MAPSTER stores all metadata locally. Using ArcCatalog™, OHEB's GIS Unit prepared a comprehensive set of Federal Geographic Data Committee complaint metadata. Clicking on a hyperlinked spatial data layer name presents metadata documents in HTML format. Users also can save metadata documents on their computers.

Similarly, any Web map service that supports these standards can access and integrate data presented through MAPSTER. Compliance not only expands the range of available data but also lets users more easily access and integrate data as hosted services, eliminating the need for data conversion. If users do not want to access the system through a hosted service, MAPSTER provides a data download function. The GIS Unit's Spatial Data Holding Web pages allow download of OHEB data in shapefile format. MAPSTER links users to the relevant custodian's site if the data comes from outside OHEB.

Building the MAPSTER portal

MAPSTER uses ArcIMS 9.0 for Internet mapping services. The OHEB GIS unit developed the portal interface in Moxi Media™ Internet Mapping Framework (IMF) for OpenGIS®. This Java™/JSP development environment permitted rapid customization, allowing the GIS unit to build and deploy MAPSTER in just three months. Interface design focused on the requirements of OHEB staff for swift, hassle-free access to key datasets. The application design aimed to provide an intuitive interface, as the majority of users would have little or no specific training in GIS or the portal. Data searching, integration, and visualization tools had to be presented in a clear and simple manner.

Providing data and tools needed for the task at hand

The result is a highly structured application portal. A directory tree presents spatial data layers under a logical nested directory structure. Users work with this in a way similar to navigating a Windows® Explorer directory. The tree contains four broad directories (Thematic Layers, Image Layers, BC Base Map Layers, and Yukon Base Map Layers). Underneath, a series of subdirectories hold specific datasets. The tree lets users easily turn layers on or off and access related metadata. Users must have some idea of where data appears within the structured directory, and portal managers must update it when they add new data. Future enhancements will incorporate an OGC compliant metadata search engine that supports keyword and geographic searches for data, not only throughout the OHEB and DFO but also across international spatial data infrastructures. This functionality will reduce maintenance overheads and offer fast and efficient access to hundreds of spatial datasets that are now difficult to locate or access.

The map service provides tools that allow easy map navigation. Users can zoom to a town or DFO facility, scale and measure, and retrieve information on map features from related textual databases. Staff can generate simple maps using templates provided. The portal supports output of maps in PDF format and lets users e-mail them from the MAPSTER interface. Users can also generate summaries of commonly referenced statistics, for example, hatchery releases, salmon escapes, and marine resources.

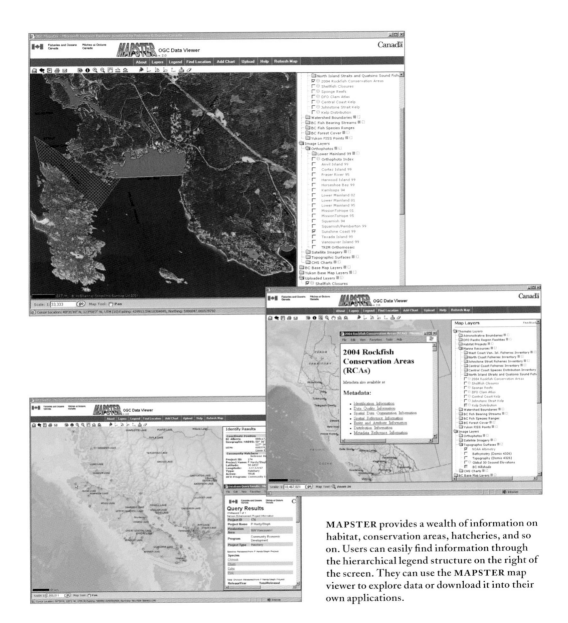

MAPSTER provides a wealth of information on habitat, conservation areas, hatcheries, and so on. Users can easily find information through the hierarchical legend structure on the right of the screen. They can use the MAPSTER map viewer to explore data or download it into their own applications.

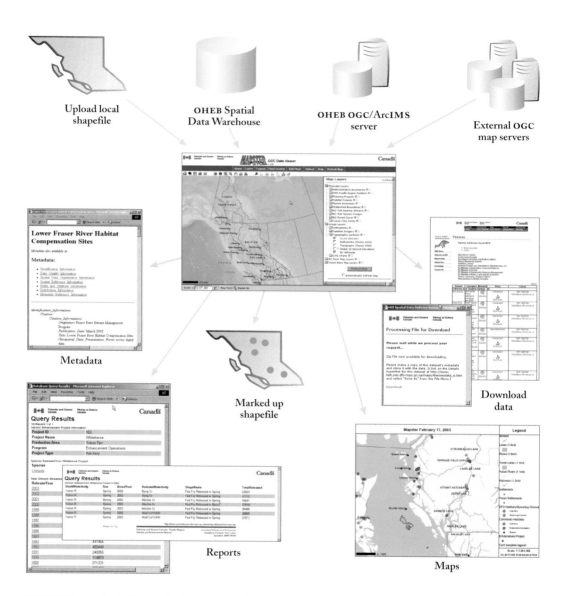

Upload local shapefile

OHEB Spatial Data Warehouse

OHEB OGC/ArcIMS server

External OGC map servers

Metadata

Marked up shapefile

Download data

Reports

Maps

MAPSTER uses ArcIMS 4.0.1 for Internet mapping services, taking advantage of its WMS and Web Feature Service (WFS) connectors to provide OGC compliance. OHEB's GIS unit developed the portal interface in Moxi Media Internet Mapping Framework (IMF) for OpenGIS. This Java/JSP development environment permits rapid customization and allowed the GIS unit to build and deploy MAPSTER in just three months.

In addition, the portal permits basic graphical data entry and lets users add their own datasets. Interface tools allow users to create points, lines, or polygons and then save the features in ESRI shapefile format or include them in map output. Staff members can add their own data files, for example, from GPS or CAD systems, to the portal interface. MAPSTER projects such data on the fly, letting users load or view it with other datasets on the portal. OHEB users find these simple edit-and-load functions particularly relevant. The functions give users a relatively easy, inexpensive way to create their own maps and transmit and receive GIS information.

The MAPSTER portal provides a single point of access for key spatial datasets. It also offers a focused set of basic geographic functionality to explore the data while simplifying access and saving time.

Following its community-based approach, OHEB made MAPSTER available on the Internet *(www-heb.pac.dfo-mpo. gc.ca/maps/maps-data_e.htm)*. This kind of sharing supports effective, open communication with stakeholders, builds understanding of policies and programs, and encourages reviews of the Branch's work. Community and stakeholder involvement helps safeguard the habitats and fisheries in the vast region of Pacific Canada. The MAPSTER portal plays its part by promoting access to essential datasets, presentation, and analytical tools.

CHAPTER 7

SCAN:
Public health information
in South Carolina

Health is a common concern the world over, whether securing clean water for a village, combating the latest flu epidemic, or pressing for an investigation into cancer clusters. Protecting our communities, our families, and ourselves depends on our ability to receive accurate, timely information. Recent media coverage about outbreaks of the West Nile Virus and Severe Acute Respiratory Syndrome (SARS) highlighted the need for disseminating information. This includes the open exchange of data between health authorities and its prompt and effective distribution to the public. Communicating this way helps us more quickly identify patterns and causes of health threats and increases the speed, coordination, and effectiveness of control measures. It heightens public awareness and ensures people have the information they need to make informed decisions.

The South Carolina Department of Health and Environmental Control (DHEC) has developed a state-of-the-art information portal that ensures fast and efficient access to public health information. The South Carolina Community Assessment Network (SCAN) portal provides a real-time, interactive gateway to DHEC's databases. The portal allows users to integrate and analyze health data with other socioeconomic, demographic, geographic, and administrative data from local, state, and federal agencies. It provides accurate, up-to-date information to health professionals, local government agencies, academics, and the general public. The SCAN portal can be found at *scangis.dhec.sc.gov/scan.*

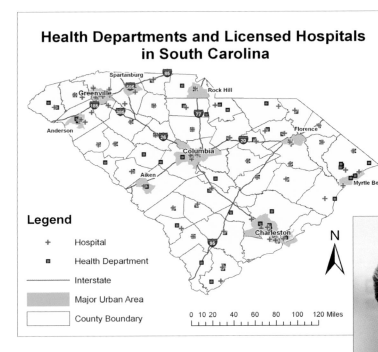

Health Departments and Licensed Hospitals in South Carolina

Legend

+   Hospital

▣   Health Department

———   Interstate

▨   Major Urban Area

▭   County Boundary

0 10 20   40   60   80   100   120 Miles

N

The Department of Health and Environmental Control has responsibility for promoting and protecting public health and the environment for over four million inhabitants of South Carolina. The department delivers services through forty-six county health departments and a network of 1,500 licensed hospitals (shown in the map above), clinics, care centers, and other health facilities.

Health services in South Carolina

DHEC is the primary public health authority in South Carolina with responsibility for promoting and protecting public health and environment statewide. It covers more than 31,000 square miles (80,290 square kilometers), containing more than four million people. The department delivers health services through forty-six county health departments organized into eight regions, which contain a network of 1,500 licensed hospitals, clinics, care centers, and other health facilities. The department regulates these facilities and advises on public health issues statewide. As part of these duties, the department collects, aggregates, and monitors health information. Data comes from many sources: neighborhood clinics, hospitals, and dispensaries; birth and death registries; and special programs and surveys. This rich data stream of spatial and nonspatial information provides the basis for monitoring health and for analyzing health disparities, disease clusters, and access-to-care issues. In-depth analysis often sheds light on underlying environmental, health, and socioeconomic risk factors and leads to the development of intervention and prevention strategies.

DHEC's Division of Biostatistics and Health GIS is responsible for analyzing and distributing this information. Users include local health professionals within and outside the department, federal agencies, academics, and interested members of the public. Before development of the portal, users had to rely on the Biostatics Division's annual reports as the primary means of data dissemination. However, these only reached a limited number of people and presented information in a rigid manner. The reports also took months to prepare and could not present information on unfolding health issues. As a result, the Biostatistics Division received many *ad hoc* requests for information and data that did not appear in the reports. Staff handled these requests individually, extracting and processing information and producing tables and maps. Often this process involved numerous iterations to help researchers narrow down their information requirements. In addition, a complex set of state, federal, and professional regulations protecting patient confidentiality, control, and release of health information required staff to scrutinize all *ad hoc* reports to ensure they met appropriate codes and standards. This consumed time, slowed delivery of information, and distracted staff from more in-depth research. DHEC needed a more efficient, robust way to provide user access and explore public health information.

Portals for health

In 2002, DHEC's Biostatistics Division launched a catalog portal that permitted access to DHEC's spatial data holdings. Users can query data holdings either by division or topic and receive data listings and metadata that meet their search criteria. Accessible through the Internet and intranet, this portal lets users either download data directly in .e00 or shapefile formats, or it provides them with the contact details of the relevant data holders. They also can access Federal Geographic Data Committee (FGDC) compliant metadata and images giving an example of each dataset. In addition to this catalog, the Biostatistics Division developed a number of stand-alone map services that let users view and build their own maps. The Community Mapper, for example, integrates raster and vector data from DHEC and other organizations, allowing users to overlay public health information on general topographic mapping and satellite or orthophoto imagery.

While these developments proved extremely popular, they provided only limited analytical capabilities. The GIS team for analytical services faced high demands from many users who did not have access to GIS or statistical software and lacked the skills to extract, manipulate, and analyze the data.

The Biostatistics Division designed SCAN to meet this demand. The portal augments rather than replaces the GIS Data Server and existing systems. The databases distributed throughout DHEC continue to store and manage different health datasets, and the catalog portal remains the primary route for retrieving entire layers of spatial information. The SCAN portal provides an integrating layer above these systems that lets users easily access and integrate data within them and create graphs, thematic maps, and other needed analyses. The SCAN portal kept disruption to established data management programs to a minimum, making them available to others and maximizing the benefits derived from them.

Requests

(Birth, death, infant death, population, MCH, pregnancy, PRAMS, BRFSS, cancer, lead poisoning)

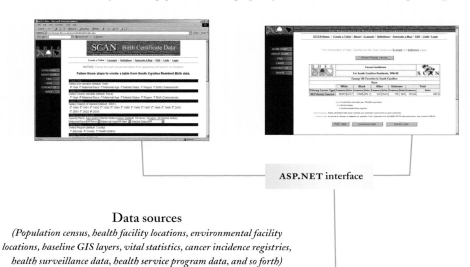

Data sources

(Population census, health facility locations, environmental facility locations, baseline GIS layers, vital statistics, cancer incidence registries, health surveillance data, health service program data, and so forth)

SCAN portal

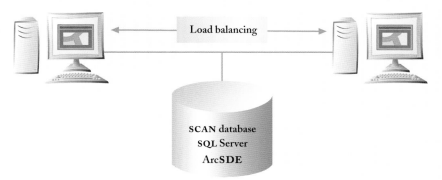

Using standards-based Internet technology, SCAN is built on the ASP.NET environment and with ESRI ArcIMS for Internet mapping and Microsoft SQL Server/ArcSDE for data management. Health data is drawn from a variety of databases (Oracle, SQL Server, and DB2®) distributed throughout DHEC. Interface design and applications development uses ASP.NET and HTML and XML for data exchange. Data from statistical and geographical results are generated on the fly using algorithms developed with ASP.NET and ArcIMS. DHEC plans to expand the geospatial functionality by moving the system into an ArcGIS Server environment. Use of cutting-edge COTS tools and IT standards helped ensure rapid, cost-effective development.

Output

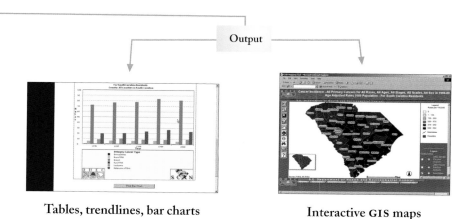

Tables, trendlines, bar charts   Interactive GIS maps

The modular approach

The SCAN portal adopts a modular design, with each module focusing on a particular dataset or health issue. Modules, for example, cover birth and death statistics, incidents of cancer or lead poisoning, and mothers' health and lifestyles. Each module contains a wealth of information about the topic and other data (socioeconomic, administrative, topographic datasets) that may help interpretation and analysis.

The modular approach permitted DHEC to develop highly tailored interfaces for each topic. The interfaces lead users through the complex steps of extracting and presenting information from DHEC databases. The interfaces let users select variables and year (or combination of years) to study, define how to aggregate or group data (by variable, or geographic ZIP Code, county, district, or state), and decide what statistical operations to apply. Users can then select whether to present the statistics in table, bar chart, or trendline formats, or as maps. In developing the modular interface, the SCAN development team and their consultants worked closely with health officers, statisticians, and epidemiologists throughout the department to ensure the interface and steps in each module were clearly defined and accurate. A data custodian is associated with each module and has overall responsibility for the data featured in the module, interface design, and access issues. The SCAN development team ensured all modules had the same basic structure, look, and feel. Once users learn to use a chart or map in one module, they can use similar features in other modules with ease.

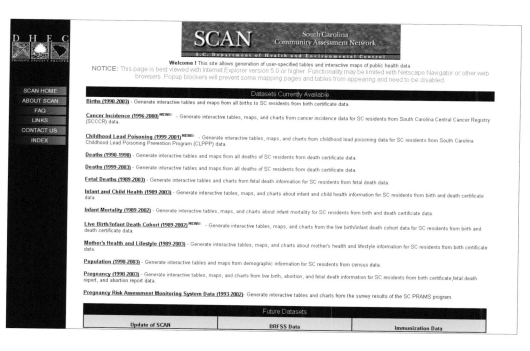

SCAN
South Carolina
Community Assessment Network
S.C. Department of Health and Environmental Control

Welcome ! This site allows generation of user-specified tables and interactive maps of public health data.
NOTICE: This page is best viewed with Internet Explorer version 5.0 or higher. Functionality may be limited with Netscape Navigator or other web browsers. Popup blockers will prevent some mapping pages and tables from appearing and need to be disabled.

SCAN HOME
ABOUT SCAN
FAQ
LINKS
CONTACT US
INDEX

Datasets Currently Available

Births (1990-2003) - Generate interactive tables and maps from all births to SC residents from birth certificate data.

Cancer Incidence (1996-2000) NEW - Generate interactive tables, maps, and charts from cancer incidence data for SC residents from South Carolina Central Cancer Registry (SCCCR) data.

Childhood Lead Poisoning (1999-2001) NEW - Generate interactive tables, maps, and charts from childhood lead poisoning data for SC residents from South Carolina Childhood Lead Poisoning Prevention Program (CLPPP) data.

Deaths (1990-1998) - Generate interactive tables and maps from all deaths of SC residents from death certificate data.

Deaths (1999-2003) - Generate interactive tables and maps from all deaths of SC residents from death certificate data.

Fetal Deaths (1989-2003) - Generate interactive tables and charts from fetal death information for SC residents from fetal death data.

Infant and Child Health (1989-2003) - Generate interactive tables, maps, and charts about infant and child health information for SC residents from birth and death certificate data.

Infant Mortality (1989-2002) - Generate interactive tables, maps, and charts about infant mortality for SC residents from birth and death certificate data.

Live Birth/Infant Death Cohort (1989-2002) NEW - Generate interactive tables, maps, and charts from the live birth/infant death cohort data for SC residents from birth and death certificate data.

Mother's Health and Lifestyle (1989-2003) - Generate interactive tables, maps, and charts about mother's health and lifestyle information for SC residents from birth certificate data.

Population (1990-2003) - Generate interactive tables and maps from demographic information for SC residents from census data.

Pregnancy (1990-2003) - Generate interactive tables, maps, and charts from live birth, abortion, and fetal death information for SC residents from birth certificate, fetal death report, and abortion report data.

Pregnancy Risk Assessment Monitoring System Data (1993-2002)- Generate interactive tables and charts from the survey results of the SC PRAMS program.

Future Datasets

Update of SCAN	BRFSS Data	Immunization Data

The **SCAN** homepage *(http://scangis.dhec.sc.gov)* presents the user with a list of modules focusing on particular datasets or health issues. Modules group related data, analysis, and reporting services. The combination of services varies depending on the nature of the module and the user's access rights. **DHEC** can quickly add or modify modules to cover new surveys or current events. The modular approach requires work to establish the logic flow and server-side processes for each module. This effort, however, is easily justified by the increased access and flexibility brought to users and the dramatic reduction in *ad hoc* queries coming into **DHEC GIS** staff.

If users select to map data, the portal generates a custom choropleth map and displays it in an independent map window. All processing involved occurs on the fly, using custom components within DHEC's database and application servers. The mapping interface gives users standard pan, zoom, buffer, and query operations and lets them add data such as detailed base maps, administrative boundaries, and census statistics. For example, researchers could explore incidents of lead poisoning in children by creating a ZIP Code-level map showing the number of children whose blood lead level exceeded a user-defined ratio. They could then add information from recent census data showing median income and percent of pre-1950s homes, layers that traditionally show a strong correlation with elevated blood lead levels. Adding other layers such as health facilities and schools would allow researchers to target intervention or education programs concerning lead poisoning to areas of greatest need. Other users may, for example, investigate teenage pregnancies in different socioeconomic or ethnic groups or develop environmental risk profiles for cancer by analyzing the distribution of cases of different types or stages of cancer.

SCAN gives users the flexibility to analyze data as they wish. Users can explore the data in depth and easily rerun queries with different parameters or timeframes. It takes a couple minutes at most to define an analysis and receive the results. The modular approach allows users who often have little or no knowledge of the data or GIS and statistical techniques involved to independently explore and analyze complex datasets and issues.

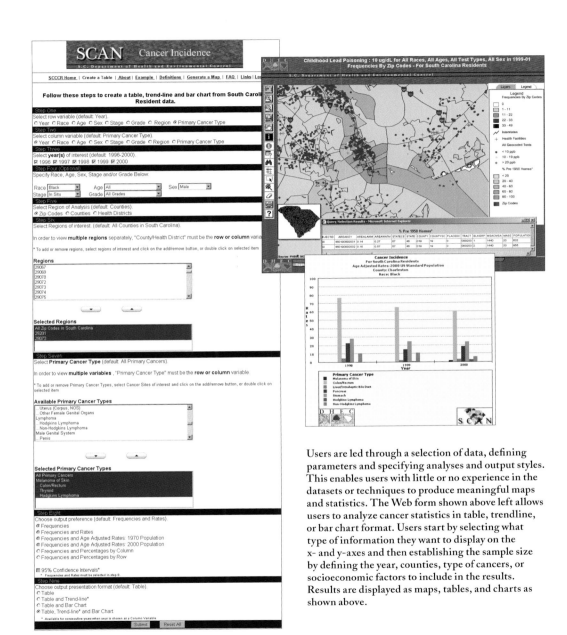

Users are led through a selection of data, defining parameters and specifying analyses and output styles. This enables users with little or no experience in the datasets or techniques to produce meaningful maps and statistics. The Web form shown above left allows users to analyze cancer statistics in table, trendline, or bar chart format. Users start by selecting what type of information they want to display on the x- and y-axes and then establishing the sample size by defining the year, counties, type of cancers, or socioeconomic factors to include in the results. Results are displayed as maps, tables, and charts as shown above.

Balancing access, security, and confidentiality

The SCAN portal also greatly increases access to health data, letting anyone with an Internet connection access the public portal interface. DHEC knew that encouraging access to information would increase the risk of misinterpretation and misuse of data. To counter this, data custodians for each module can control how SCAN presents data. They also helped author a comprehensive set of metadata for all datasets accessible through the portal and short, easy-to-understand definitions of medical and statistical variables. The development team created a network of online help, error checks, and information prompts that guide users as they define parameters and analyses, and information and tools to help users interpret the results.

In addition, the SCAN development team established a complex set of access controls to manage the data or tools available to different types of users. This is done with password protection and with session-based security that controls the level and duration of access. This allows managers to control access to entire datasets, particular variables, and even the detail in which data can be viewed by different types of users. For example, DHEC staff responsible for investigating cancer distributions can retrieve details of individual cancer cases. The public or external researchers can only access cancer statistics aggregated to ZIP Code or larger spatial unit. The system also presents Memoranda of Agreement (MOA) that users must read and accept before accessing certain datasets, helping to reinforce responsibilities and proper use of restricted data.

Formal security and access in these controls reduces the chance of inadvertent release of sensitive information and improves efficiency. Once DHEC allocates a user with access privileges, it doesn't need to check the individual reports and maps the user produced.

Many regulations and guidelines govern the collection and presentation of health data. International standards include the International Classification of Disease codes. National standards include those followed by agencies and organizations such as the Social Security Administration, the National Association of Public Health Statistics and Information Systems, and the Centers for Disease Control and Prevention. The Health Insurance Portability and Accountability Act regulates access to health data.

Impact and future

SCAN has had a dramatic impact since its launch. Statistics show more than 2,000 individual users visit the portal's homepage every month, with a monthly hit rate of more than 40,000. The system generates more than 200 tables and maps per day and has significantly decreased the number of requests for *ad hoc* reports coming into the Biostatistics Division. For example, requests from nonprofit teen pregnancy councils have decreased by 75 percent since the introduction of the module focusing on pregnancy statistics. Similarly, district and regional epidemiologists who once relied on the Biostatistics Division to generate statistics for annual health service operation plans can now do this themselves. The system dramatically improves data accessibility and response times. By working directly with the data, users can explore it more fully, find new ways to apply it, and learn more about the issues under investigation. The system saves hundreds of DHEC staff hours that would otherwise have been spent addressing these questions and allows the Biostatistics Division to concentrate on data management, complex analytical tasks, and system maintenance and expansion.

Based on SCAN's success, DHEC is expanding the portal into related projects. For example, DHEC has developed a statewide Emergency Hurricane Sheltering System and Emergency Operations Centers application based on the same architecture. These extend the portal beyond traditional public health into general security and emergency response coordination. The sheltering system gives authorities up-to-date status of each shelter facility and provides the public with driving instructions from their current location to the nearest shelter. The multiagency system involves county and state level emergency management services, the Department of Social Services, and the American Red Cross. The portal provides an integrated environment for fast, effective, and coordinated action.

Ongoing work will align SCAN with the Centers for Disease Control and Prevention's plans for a Public Health Information Network (PHIN). This federal system will link state public health systems to create a national system for communicating public health information. In this way SCAN helps the DHEC not also only serve citizens of South Carolina but also participate in a federal health information framework that will span the nation.

CHAPTER 8

I2M portal:
Managing U.S. Navy
Atlantic Fleet installations

Web-based spatial portals attract organizations that own and manage large, widely dispersed property portfolios. Portals provide a central, spatially aware interface to asset records throughout an organization. Designing and building portals promotes communication between remote and site-based asset managers and serves as a catalyst to coordinate wider business processes and operations. The U.S. Navy discovered this during development of its Integrated Installation Management (I2M) system, a secure Web-based asset management portal for shore-based facilities of the Atlantic Fleet.

The Atlantic Fleet operates approximately twenty-four installations along the Atlantic coast of the United States. Installations include harbors, airfields, training grounds, command centers, and living quarters. The fleet's more than 25,000 facilities range from buildings, docks, and repair yards to roads, walls, and fences. The portfolio includes nationally important historical buildings, state-of-the art dry dock and engineering facilities, high-tech communication and command posts, and top security locations. Replacing them would cost billions of U.S. dollars.

Managing maintenance

Each installation maintains its own facilities. Maintenance budgets, however, are controlled centrally. Fleet headquarters keeps track of facilities' conditions and reviews and authorizes all maintenance budgets. Fleet headquarters requires installations to report annually on facility conditions. Their submissions identify deficiencies (items requiring maintenance) and estimate the resources needed to fix them. The reports require timely, accurate, and consistent information from all installations. This strategically important process goes beyond simple asset management and financial control. The Navy needs current condition status of its facilities to monitor installation readiness and plan operations.

In the past, gathering asset condition took too long and required lots of labor. To complete their reports, inspectors referred to plans and as-built drawings, reports of previous inspections and work, and many other pieces of information. The Fleet had no central repository to hold the information. Different groups held data in different, often incompatible formats. In any one installation, inspectors might need to gather information from many CAD, GIS, database, and hardcopy filing systems in different sections and offices. Inspectors often took weeks to consolidate a consistent picture of asset status at each installation.

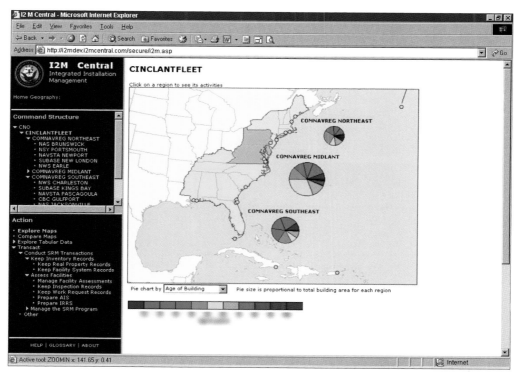

Certain areas of the images shown in this chapter have been blurred for security reasons.

The Atlantic Fleet is organized into three regional commands: Northeast, Mid-Atlantic, and Southeast. The Atlantic Fleet manages installations along the entire Atlantic seaboard of the United States. Facilities range from harbors and airbases to sports facilities and museums. Together, these facilities might record as many as twenty-five thousand maintenance items annually.

Property managers at regional and central headquarters had similar problems, as installation reports varied in style and content. Verifying and then consolidating reports into a Fleet-wide assessment often added at least two months to the cumbersome process. Problems appearing after the annual inspections and ongoing maintenance went unrecorded until the next annual survey. Central planners found it impossible to confirm current facility status throughout the Fleet with any confidence.

An internal audit conducted in 2000 highlighted these problems and led to the development and launch of the I2M spatial portal.

Design criteria

System design focused on several key criteria. The Navy needed a system that would present current, comprehensive, and consistent status information throughout the Fleet. Wherever possible, I2M would mine data from existing applications and systems. Using existing systems would avoid the massive disruption and cost involved in installing a completely new fleet-wide asset management system. It also retained the autonomy of installations to manage their own data. The system must also be accessible and secure. I2M would handle sensitive information, including detailed site maps, building floor plans, and facility condition reports for many sensitive locations. The system must keep this information secure yet allow access from authorized staff throughout the Fleet and possibly, the wider national defense organization.

Building the I2M application portal

Applied Geographics, Inc. (AppGeo) of Boston, Massachusetts, led application design and development. AppGeo worked with a facilities engineering firm, Unity Consultants, of Burke, Virginia, to provide project supervision and expertise in asset management. Starting in March 2001, the team created a prototype portal within three months. From August 2001 until project completion in August 2004, a structured program of 24 releases, one every six weeks, incrementally added data, functionality, and security controls and responded to user feedback.

This intensive release cycle was an important part of project implementation. The team worked alongside more than thirty Navy representatives drawn from each installation and from regional and central headquarters. Fleet command headquarters also established a Configuration Control Board (CCB) to represent each region and Navy Fleet headquarters. System development and its long-term success required the consensus of project and board members based throughout the eastern United States. This made regular face-to-face meetings of the entire group impossible. But the team launched the portal early and sustained a rapid release cycle, creating a channel for ideas on design, functionality, interfaces, and standard business practices to flow. The portal drove the project, bringing together team members, stimulating debate, and providing early proof of the project's benefits and goals.

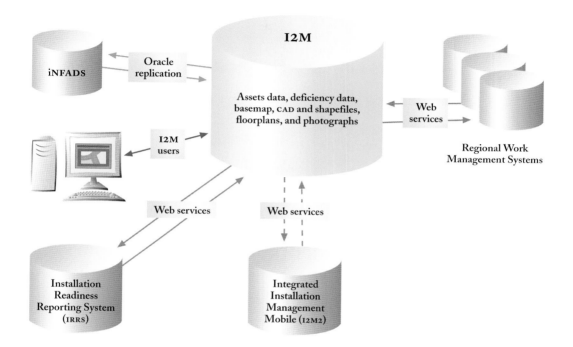

The **I2M** accesses data from a central data repository. The repository is constantly managed and updated and holds current facility condition status throughout the Fleet. A number of harvesting techniques collect data from different systems. Some use database replication; others use automated Web services triggered when changes are made to the remote databases.

I2M is a highly structured application portal that revolves around a central data repository. The repository holds asset inventory, deficiency data (status, work, and budget requirements, work progress and so on), geospatial data (location plans and site maps of the installations), and other related information such as floor plans, images, and documents. I2M's search, view, and analysis functions access this repository. I2M maintains the data in the repository by mining data from other systems. A series of Web services and automated Extraction, Transformation, and Load tools routinely harvest and consolidate data from different installations. Creating a central data repository duplicates data yet also allows the Navy to control portal performance and security.

Data-harvesting approaches vary, depending on the source databases. Database replication routines across secure connections copy textual data from the Navy's central asset databases. In a couple of the Fleet's regions, Web services extract and transfer deficiency data between servers. These use eXtensible Markup Language (XML) as the common exchange. One region uses I2M as its central database and enters deficiency data directly into the system. The development team created a dedicated Web interface that allowed authorized users at each installation in the region to log on and maintain their datasets directly within the I2M repository.

The system also links to regional applications that manage work orders. Once Fleet headquarters approves work proposals, the portal automatically passes details about the job to regional work order management systems. These in turn update I2M as work progresses, ensuring continuous updates of condition status within the repository.

Benefits and future

I2M improves consistency across Fleet systems and automates much of the conversion and consolidation of datasets from different systems and installations. The team restricted modifications to adding fields to certain datasets and synchronizing classification schemes. A single, commonly understood definition of a deficiency appeared as I2M development progressed. Agreement followed on business rules and algorithms on classifying and setting priorities for deficiencies.

A major project accomplishment was the collection of relevant GIS data from each installation. Data varied in format, scale, completeness, and accuracy. The team created a single, rationalized base mapping dataset based on supplied data, adding metadata to track the source and processing steps. This eliminated many concerns with the original datasets, including unclosed building footprints, incompatible georeferencing systems, duplicate lines, and overshoots. It also established system-wide identifiers to link map features to the Navy's asset and deficiency datasets. I2M uses this dataset for all GIS operations. The Navy adopted the first Fleet-wide geospatial dataset to provide a consistent base map of all installations. The dataset also serves other Fleet-wide operational systems.

The I2M portal provides a single integrated interface to facility asset information. For users at regional and Fleet headquarters, the portal provides rapid access to consistent, up-to-date facility information. Within installations, users like the convenience of one-stop shopping to get relevant data from discrete systems in the site.

Users interact with the portal through a series of different Web pages designed for specific business processes and authority levels. Upon successful authorization, users select a geography or level of organization to explore (the Navy restricts access to information at some levels). They retrieve information on current or historical status reports, work activities, and financial details, as well as detailed accounts of inspection and work history for particular facilities. Users can access asset databases through a graphical map-based interface or seek information through textual queries. The map interface also shades facilities thematically, based on a range of parameters including condition status, age, value, responsibility, and maintenance cost. Reports aggregate this information to installation or regional levels, offering users a clear picture of the spatial distribution of facility condition, cost effectiveness, performance, and so on.

In addition, the portal serves data directly to a number of systems within and outside the Navy. This includes providing facility status information to the Department of Defense's Installation Readiness Reporting System (IRRS) and map data to the Navy's GeoReadiness Center.

I2M provides direct access to an integrated repository of facility status and maintenance information harvested from systems at each installation or regional command. Data is served directly to a number of applications or can be analyzed through specifically tailored Web pages.

I2M portal: Managing U.S. Navy Atlantic Fleet installations

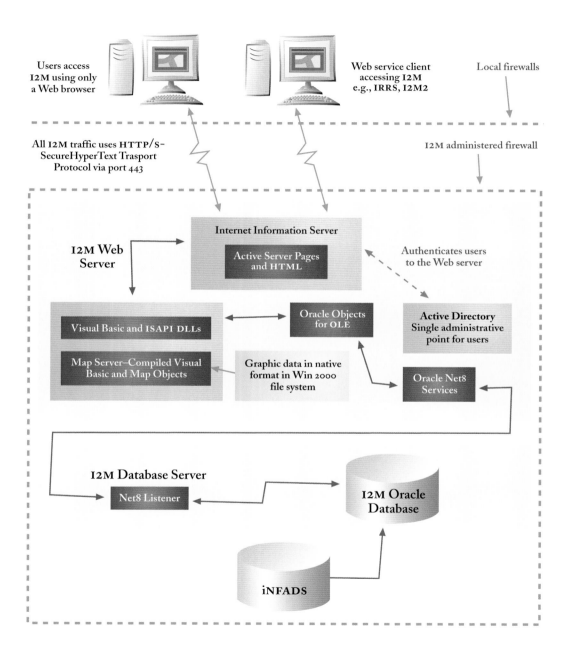

Users access
I2M using only
a Web browser

Web service client
accessing I2M
e.g., IRRS, I2M2

Local firewalls

All I2M traffic uses HTTP/S–
SecureHyperText Trasport
Protocol via port 443

I2M administered firewall

**I2M Web
Server**

Internet Information Server

Active Server Pages
and HTML

Authenticates users
to the Web server

Visual Basic and ISAPI DLLs

Oracle Objects
for OLE

Active Directory
Single administrative
point for users

Map Server–Compiled Visual
Basic and Map Objects

Graphic data in native
format in Win 2000
file system

Oracle Net8
Services

I2M Database Server

Net8 Listener

**I2M Oracle
Database**

iNFADS

The portal uses a dual Web and database server configuration. Hardware resides in a secure data center. The system runs Microsoft Windows 2000, Microsoft Internet Information Server 5.0, and uses Active Directory for authentication. Data is stored in the Oracle 8i™/7 Enterprise Edition. The system accesses all CAD and GIS data in its native file formats, including AutoCAD drawing file format for floor plans and ESRI shapefile format for basemap data. The interface uses ESRI MapObjects® Internet Mapping Server (MO/IMS). System design conforms to the Department of Defense Information Technology Security and Accreditation Process (DITSCAP). It uses roles-based authentication throughout to determine data and functionality access privileges. In addition, it uses data encryption and Secure Socket Layer (SSL) connections with public key interface to secure data transfer.

I2M received full authority to operate in November 2002, adhering to the Department of Defense Information Technology Security and Accreditation Process (DITSCAP) requirements. Throughout the development cycle, the portal let project members discuss, evaluate, and ultimately agree on consistent definitions and classification. The portal now provides a suite of automated and semiautomated data harvesting Web services that help eliminate redundancies in entering, collecting, and synchronizing facility and maintenance information. I2M handles collection, consolidation, and dissemination of information to authorized staff or systems. And the portal helps staff make better-informed business and strategic decisions. Acting as a data broker sitting on top of existing systems, the portal secures existing investments in technology and skills while providing the integration and consolidation that was previously lacking. Based on the lessons learned and the successes of the I2M system, the Navy is planning a new portal that will cover the Pacific and Atlantic Fleets.

CHAPTER 9

GeoInfo One-Stop:
Hong Kong's planning
information portal

Effective communication is essential for state and city planning departments. They must listen to, understand, and reconcile the needs of various stakeholders during the preparation of land-use zoning plans and regulations. Stakeholders often have many competing interests regarding health and safety, security, the environment, cultural and historical heritage, social welfare, industry, and commerce. Equally important, planning departments must ensure that land-use plans and the decisions based on them are open, transparent, and accessible. Stakeholders need the opportunity to review plans and decisions and offer feedback. And the plans must be flexible enough to respond to the changing needs of the local area and community. Planning is a process of consultation, debate, and compromise.

In the past, planners published zoning maps and planning application rulings in newspapers or displayed them in libraries and other civic buildings. Today, the Internet and particularly Internet mapping are increasingly augmenting traditional methods as modern technology becomes more powerful and accessible. The Planning Department (PlanD) of the Hong Kong Special Administrative Region, China, recently unveiled a one-stop spatial portal that gives other government departments and the public fast, efficient access to land-use planning information. Stakeholders can find zoning plans, planning applications, decisions, and objections. The portal provides a new and powerful way for PlanD to reach out to stakeholders and encourage clear, open dialog on the future shape of Hong Kong.

Planning in Hong Kong

Planners face many challenges in Hong Kong. Home to about 6.8 million people, Hong Kong occupies a land area of just under 1,100 square kilometers (424 square miles). This includes more than 260 small outlying islands and large areas of steep, hilly terrain unsuitable for urban or economic development. More than a third of the area falls within designated Country Parks that protect undeveloped land for nature conservation and outdoor recreation. Pressure to develop areas for urban and economic development put intense demand on these lands. Partly for that reason, Hong Kong has some of the highest population densities in the world. Forecasts indicate that population will continue to rise, placing further demands on scarce resources. Hong Kong's place as one of Asia's leading cities and a major entry point to China's dynamic economy means that the city is constantly exposed to change. Hong Kong faces continuous pressure to ensure that its transport network, financial centers, residential and business real estate, telecommunications, industrial, commercial, and recreation facilities keep pace with rapidly changing demands while serving the community's long-term interests.

Competition for land is intense in Hong Kong. Roads and tramlines weave through dense urban areas where residential, recreational, industrial, and commercial land uses jostle for space. Outside the urban area, Hong Kong is made up of steep, forested hills and numerous islands that are unsuitable for development. The Tsing Ma bridge, above left, opened in 1997 and connects Hong Kong's largest island, Lantau, to the rest of the city. The bridge permitted the relocation of Hong Kong's international airport to Lantau island and opened up the north shore of the island for urban development.

PlanD is responsible for the preparation of various town plans to guide the proper use and development of land in Hong Kong. These plans range from detailed layout plans for individual districts to development strategies for the entire territory. PlanD also provides services to the Town Planning Board (TPB), including the preparation of statutory plans (e.g., Outline Zoning Plans) that form the basis for planning control and show proposed land use and the types of activities and buildings permitted in a given area. Made up of senior government representatives and members of the local community, TPB oversees the preparation and application of plans. The Board meets regularly to consider applications for planning permission and objections or proposed revisions to statutory plans.

Hong Kong has more than one hundred statutory land-use plans ranging in scales from (1:2500–1:20,000). PlanD continually refines the plans to reflect changing conditions and the TPB's latest planning intention. In any one year, it is not uncommon for the department to make changes to more than half the plans. Amendments range from minor changes within a single zone to completely redrawing a plan.

Digital plans

One of the early adopters of GIS in Hong Kong, PlanD has used the technology extensively since the early 1990s. The department produced its first digital statutory plans in 1997. Maintaining plans in digital format made it far easier to keep plans current. The department also started geocoding planning applications and TPB's decisions. This meant that planners processing an application could quickly retrieve appropriate statutory plans, relevant planning applications, and TPB decisions.

In the past, users who wanted to access current plans would either request copies by telephone or mail, or come to PlanD offices. The ability to use digital plans opened new possibilities for disseminating data in digital format. However, only those organizations with access to GIS software could use the data. In addition, the process of circulating and maintaining numerous updates proved to be inefficient for PlanD and the user organizations.

In 2002, the department starting making statutory plans and information available through Web sites. These included a number of intranet-based systems that allowed PlanD and authorized users from other government departments to access current and archived statutory plans, records of planning enforcements, and other related information. PlanD also launched two Internet sites that provided public access to statutory plans and related archives. These sites helped PlanD explore the potential of distributed GIS and better understand user needs. However, the sites developed organically with little integration between them. Users often needed to switch between sites to collect information.

The GeoInfo One-Stop portal

PlanD's GeoInfo One-Stop portal addresses these issues by providing a unified, one-stop shop for statutory plans and related planning information. This includes planning applications and objections, requests for changes to land-use zones of statutory plans, and details of enforcement actions relating to land-use contraventions. The portal brings together datasets from different systems and provides search and presentation tools for users to explore data in new and powerful ways.

The GeoInfo One-Stop portal uses standards-based Internet technology. The portal is built on a Windows 2000 Server and the Microsoft .NET environment and uses Java 2 and ArcIMS 4.0.1 for Web development. The system is hosted on a dual system and comprises two Web servers, four map servers, and two spatial data servers. Data is maintained in ArcSDE 8.3 running on an Oracle 9i™ database. The GeoInfo One-Stop and the Statutory Planning portals share the basic architecture, data, and many of the same menu interfaces and functions, making them easy to maintain and expand.

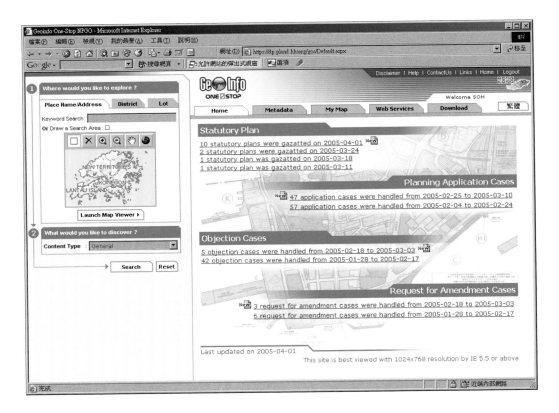

The portal homepage provides efficient search tools, allowing users to define the information they need. Links on the right side alert the user to newly updated statutory plans, planning applications, objections, and so on. Tabs along the top permit users to access metadata search functions, set their own map preferences, and register to use the portal's Web services or download data.

The flexible, user-friendly search interface illustrates the portal's value. PlanD was acutely aware that different users work with land-use records in different ways. Within government, more than forty different departments and bureaus routinely access statutory planning data. The information used to initiate a search and the information needed for retrieval varies greatly. For instance, the Environmental Protection Department may need to find planning permissions within a general area, while the Rating and Valuation Department may already know the exact lot number of the property to check. The portal lets users define a search area by geographic coordinates, an address, a commonly used place name, an administrative area, or a lot number, or simply by drawing the area on a map. The interface leads users through the process of defining their search area, providing context-sensitive quick-pick lists as the search narrows.

Similarly, users can precisely define what they want the system to return. A planner who knows the reference number of a particular application can retrieve information for this particular case. A surveyor interested in a particular building can enter the building address and receive a list of all related applications, comments, or objections. Engineers commenting on a planning application can use the system to retrieve decisions made on previous applications that might have bearing on the case. They could, for example, retrieve recent decisions on planning applications in the same area or search for applications with similar conditions (for example, applications that occur in the same land-use zone and involve a similar type of development). These tools make it easy and efficient for government users to mine PlanD's databases and help ensure the consistency and transparency in government's response to planning applications.

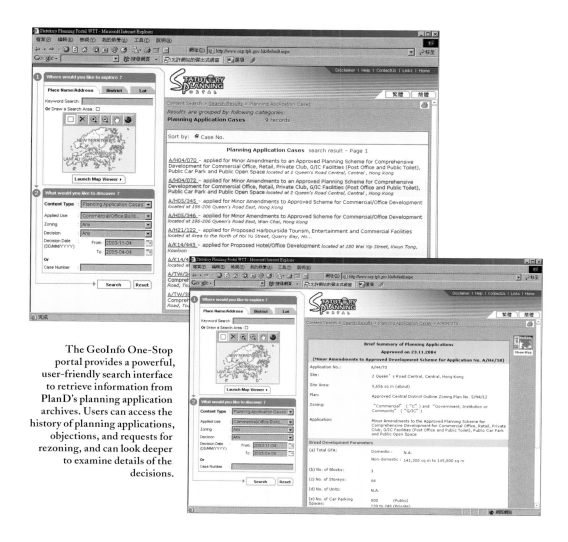

The GeoInfo One-Stop portal provides a powerful, user-friendly search interface to retrieve information from PlanD's planning application archives. Users can access the history of planning applications, objections, and requests for rezoning, and can look deeper to examine details of the decisions.

A personalized map interface

Users can view the results of searches within the portal's map interface. The map interface highlights selected features and allows users to add base maps, statutory plans, and other layers such as orthophotos, population projections, and development plans. Users can turn on and off map layers and change their display order and their transparency. They can save map parameters and preferences and reproduce maps later if necessary. Other tools allow users to save maps as image files and e-mail them from the portal interface or save them to disk.

The map interface highlights search results. The interface provides a user-friendly tool to build and query maps. Users can change the look and feel of the map by adding or removing layers and changing layer transparency and the drawing order. The system allows users to add zoning plans, population projections, and other development plans. Users can retrieve planning information related to a particular building or zone by clicking on the map feature.

Expanding Web services

For users without GIS tools, the Web map provides a simple, easy-to-use map interface. Many government departments, however, still need to use statutory plans and related planning data within their own GIS systems. For these users, the portal exposes certain map and search functions as Web services. Web services use international standards including eXtensive Markup Language (XML), Simple Object Access Protocol (SOAP), Web Services Definition Language (WSDL), and Universal Description, Discovery, and Integration (UDDI). Services range from simple map services that display current statutory plans to search tools that can, for example, take a building address and return a text file with details of planning information relating to the building. This allows GIS users in other departments to integrate and use PlanD's resources within their own GIS systems without duplicating data or recreating functionality. This is efficient and helps ensure that all government departments use the same current plans and information.

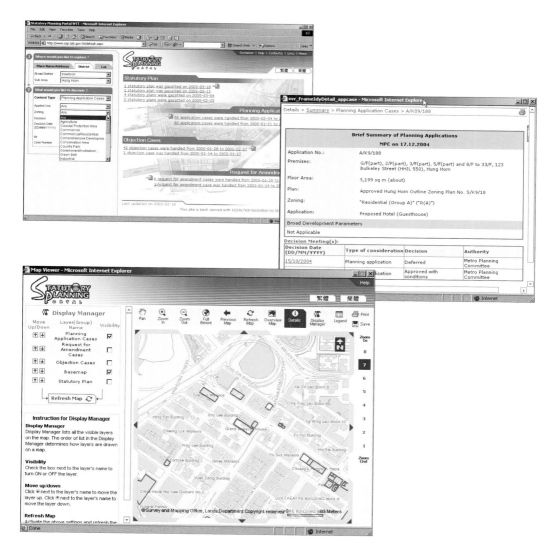

The Statutory Planning portal *(www.ozp.tpb.gov.hk)* presents many of the functions of the GeoInfo One-Stop to the public.

Access for the public

PlanD initially launched the GeoInfo One-Stop portal for use within government. In March 2005, PlanD released a public access Internet-based version. The Statutory Planning portal *(www.ozp.tpb.gov.hk)* allows the planning industry and public to access zoning plans and planning application archives. The interface and many of the functions and datasets within this portal are identical to those of the GeoInfo One-Stop. The public can access statutory plans, planning application records, and requests for land-use changes. Improving access to this information raises awareness and understanding about land-use policy and helps the public to submit more informed planning applications. The portal gives PlanD another way to contact the community it serves, promoting openness, dialog, and public involvement in the planning process.

CHAPTER 10

*Shell's global portals:
Connecting a global
enterprise*

Royal Dutch Shell, generally known as Shell, operates in more than 145 countries, locating, producing, and bringing energy and petrochemicals to market a global business. This makes it a spatial business: its main drivers include the location and accessibility of natural resources and their proximity to physical infrastructure and global markets. It is no surprise then that maps and GIS are central to many of Shell's projects. A GIS user since the 1980s, the company recently launched several spatial portals to help its staff around the world find, share, and analyze information.

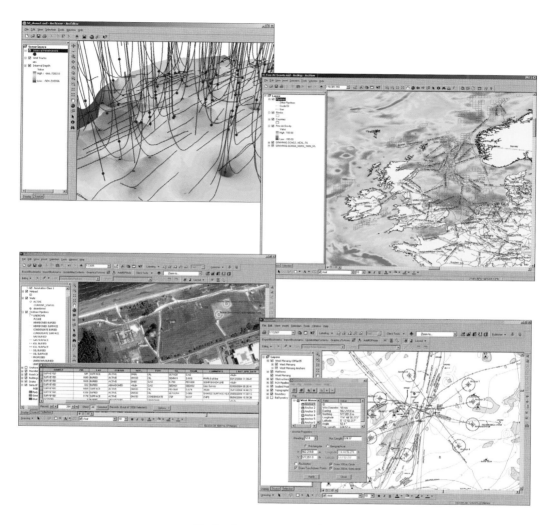

Shell makes extensive use of GIS to explore subsurface geology and search for oil reserves. The examples above show at the top left a 2.5D visualization of oil wells and an oil-bearing structure in Oman, and at the top right an analysis of anomalies in the earth's gravity in the North Sea. Shell also uses GIS for site planning at oil wells and for asset management, as is shown in the lower images from Shell's Brunei installation.

Spatial data and the energy industry

Shell is a perfect example of how GIS supports every part of the energy business, from exploration to decommissioning. Company geologists use GIS to compile regional overviews of existing or potential oil and gas reservoirs. Engineers employ GIS to position drilling rigs, locate wind farms, and manage maintenance of infrastructure in remote deserts. Environmental scientists use GIS to monitor emissions, wildlife, and biodiversity. The legal staff relies on GIS to keep landowners informed of activities affecting their properties. Shell's senior management and stakeholders receive project updates through 3D GIS displays in virtual reality rooms.

GIS and geospatial data provide the framework that ensures everything is in the right place—on the map and in the field. In the energy industry, failure of this framework can have serious consequences. Choosing unsuitable map projections in planning an intercontinental pipeline can invalidate estimates of length, construction cost, and completion date. Omission or misplacement of pipes or service lines on maps can damage or duplicate existing ones. Confusion over coordinate systems can result in drilling in the wrong place, either outside concession areas or through unknown geological formations. Such mistakes can lead to litigation, wasted investment, and more seriously, potential threats to the environment and human lives. Safeguarding the integrity of geospatial data is therefore critical.

Justifying portals

For Shell, developing robust spatial portals is one way of securing this framework and ensuring staff access to it. Portals reduce the risk of staff missing vital information or using wrong or old data and increase the probability of spotting new trends and business opportunities that would otherwise go unnoticed. Using portals reduces time spent searching for information, giving staff more time to use it. This is important because of the huge data volumes in the energy industry. Data comes from many sources and locations worldwide and in many spatial and nonspatial, structured and unstructured formats. In the past, staff might spend more than a third of its time just looking for necessary information. Reducing search times by even half can produce significant cost savings. With a few thousand people looking for and sharing much of the same data globally, annual cost savings can easily reach millions of dollars.

Reducing costs, minimizing risk, and increasing the chance of new opportunities present a powerful business case for spatial portals.

Managing data

For portals to deliver these benefits, however, the GIS teams in Shell's Exploration and Production division (Shell EP) realized they needed an effective spatial data management strategy. Without this in place, portals could actually increase the risk of scientists finding and using dated or improperly validated datasets or getting bogged down in the wealth of information that the portal exposes.

Data management is a major challenge for energy companies. Scientists must create many versions of the same dataset as it goes through processing and analysis. Temporal data is relevant, as the company must store information on a site from the initial prospecting stage through planning, construction, production, and eventual decommissioning phases. This introduces major issues with legacy data, as much of the older information remains either in hardcopy or archive tape format. Staff must (re-)digitize such information to bring it online in a structured manner. And offices and field stations around the world use and produce data daily in different technical, administrative, and legal environments. Some countries, for example, do not allow data transfer to a neighboring country, even if the same company operates in both. Shell's Information Management principles stipulate that data must be managed and of known quality, accessible, shared, and yet secure—all at the same time.

SHELL EP DATA MANAGERS BASE THEIR APPROACH TO DATA ON FIVE GUIDING PRINCIPLES:

- Information is a business asset—so it must be managed.
- Information is a valuable—so it must be secure.
- Information is the key to growth—so it must be shared.
- Information is used—so it must be of known quality.
- Information is necessary—so it must be accessible.

Early developments

In 1994, Shell EP introduced a single corporate GIS platform. This established standards for key datasets, including topography, reservoirs, wells, pipelines, license areas, seismic survey locations, and environmental and legal information. However, maintaining the corporate platform proved difficult. It relied on a heavily customized interface supported by a small group of programmers. As interest in GIS grew throughout the company in the late 1990s, users wanted more data, new functionality, better performance, and a more integrated system. They wanted GIS to become more flexible and mainstream.

In 1999, Shell EP shifted emphasis from creating a standard GIS tool or interface toward developing corporate spatial data stores—bringing integration at the database level. With this move, the division hoped to ensure effective corporate control over spatial data and provide needed user flexibility by letting offices select and use whatever analysis application they wished. Shell adopted a single independent or neutral spatial database standard, which most application software could read. Database managers established different views of the database to support different client applications and data requirements. There was no need to copy and translate standard datasets between projects. The team that created the data would store and maintain it in the neutral database format, and users could choose the software to access the data.

In theory, this approach to data management presented an ideal solution. It provided efficient data storage without duplication and permitted different offices or projects to work with the data using the most appropriate tools. In reality, however, performance and stability remained constant problems, and maintaining the neutral database proved complex and costly. Skilled programmers had to continually update database settings to accommodate new datasets and upgrades to client applications. Data display speed also suffered in graphic applications like GIS, as the neutral storage format tended to be less efficient than the proprietary offerings by the client vendors. These factors limited the effectiveness of the neutral or open database architecture.

Development of three-tier data management

The current approach uses a three-tier data management strategy. This takes advantage of developments in the IT industry that have largely bypassed integrating data in a single database. State-of-the-art GIS software now enables direct real-time read and write between different formats, making it unnecessary to standardize on a single data format within the database. In addition, portals and Web services make it much easier to transfer and share remote data between different Web or desktop applications. Shell EP's GIS teams are moving toward integrating data at the application (client) level rather than at the database level, linking basic attributes in the GIS layers to datasets elsewhere and using the application to resolve data translation issues.

These developments allow the division to establish the three-tier data management strategy. In the first tier, a single master database stores a copy of spatial data within the company. This consists of one master database at the corporate headquarters to store global datasets and a database located at major offices worldwide to store detailed local datasets. This federated master database satisfies global and local (including legal) requirements. This authoritative collection of Shell's spatial data holdings is not only an archive but also provides information to global search and presentation applications.

The second tier consists of regional and project databases. These are flexible and cater for the specific needs of a particular project or region. Project or regional managers establish and manage such databases independently. Databases may range from collections of flat files to multiserver data archives. Project teams use them to create, edit, and check data as their work progresses. Project teams submit data to the master database once they have validated it or completed their projects. If they wish, regional and project teams can extract and store relevant data from the master database. However, these are working copies, and the data within the master database remains the official, authorized version.

The last tier in Shell's spatial data management strategy includes the increasing number of external third-party data services. Some, such as IHS Energy's hosted data services, provide industry-specific data. Others, such as the United Nations Environment Program's interactive Map Services (iMAPS) or ESRI Geography Network software, provide more general datasets. For performance reasons, Shell still deploys managed copies of such datasets on internal servers. As soon as Internet bandwidth allows, externally hosted services will replace these, thereby reducing internal data maintenance and hardware cost.

This current three-tier data management approach

- clearly defines responsibilities for data between corporate, regional, and project managers and eliminates confusion over data provenance;

- facilitates data validation, security, and backup of an authoritative database within Shell;

- allows flexibility to enable access to corporate data sources for many different end users, ranging from skilled GIS professionals to casual browsers around the world; and

- makes full use of available third-party data services to complement in-house resources.

The GIS users

Enterprise users

Web GIS application users

Desktop GIS users

Portal layer

Enterprise | Geoscience | Discovery | Other

ArcSDE Gateway

Shell Corporate Oracle Environment

GIS publication database

Live project GIS data *(personal geodatabases)*

Archive

Business databases *(science, engineering, documents, SAP, and so on)*

GIS Master Databases *(Oracle RDBMS. spatial data in either SDO_GEOMETRY or SDE_GEOMETRY)*

Load

External GIS data *(various formats)*

Spatial enabling

Spatial data within Shell EP is held in a three-tier structure. Users can access data directly from desktop applications such as ArcGIS or through a growing number of dedicated portals.

Portal development

With the data strategy in place, the Shell GIS teams rolled out the portals in late 2000. They have built targeted portals to meet specific corporate or project needs. This approach helps to control scope and avoids the (common) temptation of including too many features within a single portal. It also enables developers to tailor portals to specific requirements, providing, for example, generic keyword or catalog searches for one set of users or structured interfaces that link a number of specific datasets for another.

The Discovery Portal, for example, coordinates information on North Sea oil and gas operations for Shell offices throughout Europe. This portal integrates subsurface (textual) databases with geospatial information. It draws some datasets from the master database and others from regional- and project-based databases and electronic document management systems (EDMS). An engineer can, for example, identify a concession area on the map and check the location of different types of boreholes. The engineer can go deeper to find site reports, images of bore logs and samples, laboratory reports, contractual details, and other related information. The engineer is unaware that this data may come from half a dozen systems in multiple offices throughout the region. The logic tying the system together is in the portal itself, which uses keywords, unique feature identifiers, and a central asset register (catalog) to search and retrieve information. Prior to the launch of the Discovery Portal, staff would either have to access and use many different systems or ask data custodians to extract the data.

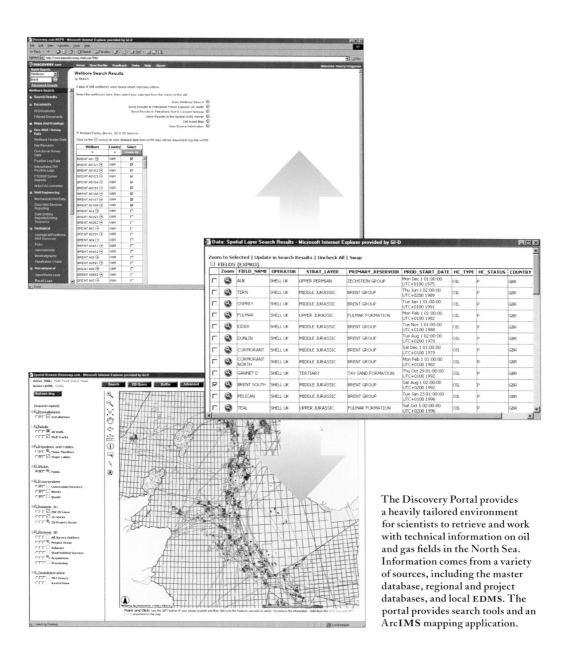

The Discovery Portal provides a heavily tailored environment for scientists to retrieve and work with technical information on oil and gas fields in the North Sea. Information comes from a variety of sources, including the master database, regional and project databases, and local EDMS. The portal provides search tools and an ArcIMS mapping application.

Based on the success of the Discovery Portal, Shell teams are extending the concept to create a Global Geoscience Portal. The new portal integrates the company's global exploration and production information with data hosted by other third-party information providers. The portal aims to make it easier for groups of international experts to work on a single project. Scientists from offices in Brazil, the United States, and the Netherlands, for example, can cooperate on a new prospect in China without leaving their desks. They access the same information, whether maps showing license boundaries, wells drilled by Shell or competitors, existing pipelines and infrastructure, detailed site reports, geological cross sections, and so on. The portal also links to a Web forum environment that lets colleagues discuss the datasets as they view them.

Senior managers can also access spatial information through Shell EP's Enterprise Portal. The Enterprise Portal integrates GIS with many other information sources, including new feeds, international industry updates, corporate information, discussion forums, administrative tools, databases, and libraries. The portal enables users to take any keyword in the GIS attribute table and submit it to the portal's federated search engine with a single click. This searches internal databases, document archives, and library catalogs as well as external sources such as contracted data vendors, trade publications, and the Internet. Based on keyword searching rather than unique identifiers, this effective approach retrieves legacy and unstructured datasets.

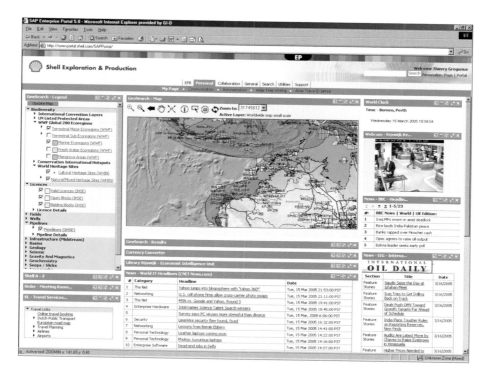

Shell EP's corporate Enterprise Portal uses SAP Enterprise technology with embedded mapping and spatial search tools. Management can access a range of spatial datasets, including base topography, asset and performance information, spatial searches, and simple analysis without leaving the portal environment. Keyword searches use the portal's federated search engine, which retrieves data from a range of sources including internal databases, documents, archives, and library catalogs as well as external contracted data vendors, trade publications, and the Internet. Because the portal uses off-the-shelf technology, internal development and maintenance is reduced to creating and maintaining the glue between the various components.

Future directions and lessons learned

Shell EP is beginning to explore ways of moving its current enterprise portals into a full corporate spatial data infrastructure (SDI). This would allow authorized users to access and search a single portal providing global GIS data and links to documents, reports, and company databases in an integrated and transparent manner. Moving the portals into an SDI requires expanding standard metadata and geocoding beyond GIS, CAD, and survey datasets to include other forms of documents.

Technology for this is now available. Operating systems, development languages, off-the-shelf GIS tools, and increasingly, robust network infrastructures all support the development of Web-based applications. Ultimately, the success of portals depends on organizational issues rather than technological ones. Bringing content to the portal requires time, effort, and money. The process includes data cleanup, agreeing on data model standards, and creating metadata. These tasks can take time in large organizations where data owners (geoscientists or business planners) are often not the same people as data custodians (GIS support or data management staff). Making portals a reality takes vision, time, dedication, buy-in, and support from all levels of the organization, but the rewards are great for organizations that rely on vast data resources. Portals provide a secure, flexible framework to access information that was once so elusive.

The case studies in this book show how spatial portals put geographic information within our reach to make better decisions that can save time, money, and even lives. Spatial portals provide the entry points to information networks that are expanding throughout organizations, cities, countries, and the international community. Today, governments and other organizations are producing data faster, more accurately, in more detail, and in greater volume than ever before. Models and analyses that help us interpret, understand, and perhaps even anticipate processes and events are becoming more flexible and sophisticated. We can benefit from this wealth of information if we make it available in a way that users can easily search, find, understand, and use. Spatial portals do this. They help us order, integrate, present, and access distributed information. Portals provide services that increase public awareness and involvement in health and environmental issues; facilitate travel, asset management, and scientific study; and help us respond more quickly to natural disasters and other emergencies.

The case studies illustrate how organizations around the world are constructing and using spatial portals. A number of common themes emerge.

Perhaps most striking is the relatively speedy construction of spatial portal sites. Many organizations had their portals up and running in a matter of months. Spatial portals are based on familiar Internet and GIS technology. Portals use common standards from the wider IT industry that underpin Internet communication, application development, and Web services. The technology is tried, tested, robust, and well understood.

Afterword

Organizations often found that the challenge in developing portals is not so much the technology but in building an environment that allows users to share services. We must adopt common standards to describe services so that users can easily understand and compare them. Service providers need encouragement to participate and maintain published metadata and services. Such an environment also requires our cooperation with user groups to identify the best ways to search and present services. Portals are only as good as their content. All organizations mentioned in the case studies stressed the need to develop good, consistent metadata, particularly with enterprise and application portals, consolidated data, and functional services. Building this environment is a time-consuming process involving multiple parties, each with its own objectives and requirements. Sharing services this way also highlights concerns about the performance and security of distributed Web services; the protection of intellectual property rights and confidential information; and the interpretation of standards, metadata, quality, and fitness for use. Until now, the lack of a single method to conceive and model spatial features and processes has made it more difficult for organizations and disciplines to share and integrate services.

These issues appear daunting. But as the case studies show, the process of building portals provides a framework that most often leads to solutions. The portals described here have enabled organizations to refine interpretation and definition of standards. They bring users and service providers together, helping them to understand each other's requirements and needs.

Vendors and the geospatial community are responding. Initiatives such as the Global Spatial Data Infrastructure (GSDI) and the Global Map project are growing and addressing these issues on an international scale. Industry groups made up of academics, vendors, and users such as the Open Geospatial Consortium have fostered generic standards. Interoperability tools allow applications to read, integrate, and write data automatically in many different formats. These tools increase flexibility and choice for users and service providers. Emerging technologies such as GIS servers support the development of distributed GIS and address concerns over performance, security, and costs involved in providing services to enterprise or Web-based users. Data-modeling initiatives are bridging differences in the ways we model the world. National SDI projects are identifying and agreeing on the format and structure of fundamental "framework" datasets. Other initiatives bring user communities together to establish generic data models for particular types of data or industries. ESRI ArcGIS® Data Models initiative, for example, establishes generic models for water and transportation industries and public land records.

We noted in the first chapter that geospatial information is key to the way we understand and respond to the world around us and that organizations often had a common interest in similar maps, datasets, and analyses. From its inception, GIS has made tremendous progress in how we model, store, analyze, and share geospatial information. Spatial portals are taking the next big step in this process by providing the gateways to the rapidly expanding network of distributed geographic information.

The ArcGIS Data Models initiative is a good example of the collaborative approach to creating generic data models. This multiagency initiative brings academic, industry, and vendors together to develop data-model templates that can be used within specific industries. These templates help users share knowledge and experience. They also help align data-modeling initiatives within a discipline and promote data sharing. For more information, visit the URL *support.esri.com/index.cfm?fa=downloads.dataModels.gateway.*

ArcXML	Arc eXtensible Markup Language
ASCII	American Standard Code for Information Interchange
ASP	Active Server Pages
CAD	computer-aided design
COTS	commercial off-the-shelf
EDMS	electronic document management system
FGDC	Federal Geographic Data Committee
GIS	geographic information system
GML	Geography Markup Language
GPS	Global Positioning System
GSDI	Global Spatial Data Infrastructure
HTML	HyperText Markup Language
HTTP	HyperText Transfer Protocol
HTTPS	HyperText Transfer Protocal (Secure)
ISO	International Organization for Standardization
JSP	JavaServer Pages
LAN	local area network

List of acronyms

NSDI	National Spatial Data Infrastructure
OGC	Open Geospatial Consortium
OGIS	Open Geodata Interoperability Specification
PDF	Portable Document Format
SDI	spatial data infrastructure
SGML	Standard Generalized Markup Language
SOAP	Simple Object Access Protocol
SQL	Structured Query Language
SSL	Secure Sockets Layer
UDDI	Universal Description, Discovery, and Integration
W3C	World Wide Web Consortium
WAN	wide area network
WFS	Web Feature Server
WMS	Web Map Server Specification
WSDL	Web Service Description Language
XML	eXtensible Markup Language

Active Server Pages (ASP)

A Microsoft server-side scripting environment that can be used to create and run dynamic, interactive Web server applications, which are typically coded in JavaScript or VBScript. An ASP file contains not only the text and HTML tags that standard Web documents contain, but also commands written in a scripting language, which can be carried out on the server.

Arc eXtensible Markup Language (ArcXML)

A file format that provides a structured method for communication between all ArcIMS components. ArcXML defines content for services and is used for requests and responses between clients, the business logic tier, and servers.

American Standard Code for Information Interchange (ASCII)

The *de facto* standard for the format of text files in computers and on the Internet. Each alphabetic, numeric, or special character is represented with a 7-bit binary number (a string of seven ones and zeros). ASCII defines 128 possible characters.

channel

An area of a Web portal that contains information about a specific topic. Channels allow portal managers to assemble and present information relevant to particular groups of users.

clearinghouse

A repository structure, physical or virtual, that collects, stores, and disseminates information, metadata, and/or data. A clearinghouse provides widespread access to information and is generally thought of as reaching or existing outside of organizational boundaries.

commercial off-the-shelf (COTS)
A type of commercial software that provides open, generic functionality which organizations can integrate with existing systems and use without having to undertake major customization.

computer-aided design (CAD)
A computer-based system for the design, drafting, and display of graphical information. Also known as computer-aided drafting, such systems are most commonly used to support engineering, planning, and illustrating activities.

data repository
See clearinghouse.

electronic document management system (EDMS)
A computer-based technology for capturing, indexing, storing, securing, and accessing data from a variety of structured and unstructured information systems.

eXtensible Markup Language (XML)
Developed by the World Wide Web Consortium, XML is a standard for designing text formats that facilitates the interchange of data between computer applications. XML is a set of rules for creating standard information formats using customized tags and sharing both the format and the data across applications.

Federal Geographic Data Committee (FGDC)
An organization established by the United States Federal Office of
Management and Budget responsible for coordinating the development,
use, sharing, and dissemination of surveying, mapping, and related spatial
data. The committee is comprised of representatives from federal and
state government agencies, academia, and the private sector. The FGDC
defines spatial data metadata standards for the United States in its Content
Standard for Digital Geospatial Metadata and manages the development of
the National Spatial Data Infrastructure (NSDI).

gazetteer
A geographic dictionary listing geographic place names and their
coordinates. Entries may include other information as well, such as area,
population, or cultural statistics. Atlases often include gazetteers, which are
used as indexes to their maps. Well-known digital gazetteers include the
U.S. Geological Survey Geographic Names Information System (GNIS) and
the Alexandria Digital Library Gazetteer.

geographic information system (GIS)
An arrangement of computer hardware, software, and geographic data that
people interact with to integrate, analyze, and visualize the data; identify
relationships, patterns, and trends; and find solutions to problems. The
system is designed to capture, store, update, manipulate, analyze, and
display the geographic information. A GIS is typically used to represent
maps as data layers that can be studied and used to perform analyses.

Geography Markup Language (GML)
An OpenGIS Implementation Specification designed to transport and store
geographic information. GML is a profile (encoding) of XML.

geoprocessing
A GIS operation used to manipulate GIS data. A typical geoprocessing
operation takes an input dataset, performs an operation on that dataset,
and returns the result of the operation as an output dataset. Common
geoprocessing operations are geographic feature overlay, feature selection
and analysis, topology processing, raster processing, and data conversion.
Geoprocessing allows for definition, management, and analysis of
information used to form decisions.

georeferencing

Aligning geographic data to a known coordinate system so it can be viewed, queried, and analyzed with other geographic data. Georeferencing may involve shifting, rotating, scaling, skewing, and in some cases warping or rubber-sheeting the data.

Global Positioning System (GPS)

A constellation of radio-emitting satellites deployed by the U.S. Department of Defense and used to determine location on the earth's surface. The orbiting satellites transmit signals that allow a GPS receiver anywhere on earth to calculate its own location through triangulation. The system is used in navigation, mapping, surveying, and other applications in which precise positioning is necessary.

Global Spatial Data Infrastructure (GSDI)

A global framework of technologies, policies, standards, and human resources necessary to acquire, process, store, distribute, and improve the utilization of geospatial data.

HyperText Markup Language (HTML)

A coding language that is a subset of SGML and is used to create Web pages for publication on the Internet. HTML is a system of tags that define the function of text, graphics, sound, and video within a document, and is now an Internet standard maintained by the World Wide Web Consortium.

HyperText Transfer Protocol (HTTP)

A protocol maintained by the World Wide Web Consortium for communication between servers and clients over the Web.

HyperText Transport Protocol (Secure) (HTTPS)

A variant of HTTP that is enhanced by a security mechanism. It allows transactions such as e-commerce and data sharing to take place on the World Wide Web in a protected way.

index
A data structure used to speed the search for records in a database or for spatial features in geographic datasets. In general, unique identifiers stored in a key field point to records or files holding more detailed information.

International Organization for Standardization (ISO)
A federation of national standards institutes from 145 countries that works with international organizations, governments, industries, businesses, and consumer representatives to define and maintain criteria for international standards.

Internet
The global network of computers that communicate through a common protocol TCP/IP.

Java
An object-oriented programming language developed by Sun Microsystems. Java provides a foundation for building and deploying cross-platform, enterprise applications.

JavaServer Pages (JSP)
A Java technology that enables rapid development of platform-independent, Web-based applications. JSP separates the user interface from content generation, enabling designers to change the overall page layout without altering the underlying dynamic content.

local area network (LAN)
Communications hardware and software that connect computers in a small area, such as a room or a building. Computers in a LAN can share data and peripheral devices, such as printers and plotters, but do not necessarily have a link to outside computers.
See also wide area network (WAN).

metadata
Information that describes the content, quality, condition, origin, and other characteristics of data or other pieces of information. Metadata for spatial data may document its subject matter; how, when, where, and by whom the data was collected; availability and distribution information; its projection, scale, resolution, and accuracy; and its reliability with regard to some standard. Metadata consists of properties and documentation. Properties are derived from the data source (for example, the coordinate system and projection of the data), while documentation is entered by a person (for example, keywords used to describe the data).

National Spatial Data Infrastructure (NSDI)
A federally-mandated framework of spatial data that refers to U.S. locations, as well as the means of distributing and using that data effectively. It includes technologies, policies, standards, and human resources necessary to acquire, process, store, distribute, and improve the utilization of geospatial data in the United States. Developed and coordinated by the FGDC, the NSDI encompasses policies, standards, and procedures for organizations to cooperatively produce and share geographic data. The NSDI is being developed in cooperation with organizations from state, local, and tribal governments; the academic community; and the private sector.

.NET
A platform for XML Web services, developed by Microsoft, which includes a toolkit for easily accessing SOAP Web services.

Open Geodata Interoperability Specification (OGIS)
A specification, developed by the Open Geospatial Consortium, Inc., to support interoperability of GIS systems in a heterogeneous computing environment.

Open Geospatial Consortium, Inc. (OGC)
An international industry consortium of companies, government agencies, and universities participating in a consensus process to develop publicly available geoprocessing specifications. Open interfaces and protocols defined by OpenGIS Specifications support interoperable solutions that "geoenable" the Web, wireless and location-based services, and mainstream IT and empower technology developers to make complex spatial information and services accessible and useful with all kinds of applications.

Portable Document Format (PDF)
A proprietary file format from Adobe that creates lightweight text-based, formatted files for distribution to a variety of operating systems.

Secure Sockets Layer (SSL)
A protocol for encrypting and transmitting private documents securely over the Internet.

service
A persistent software process that provides data or computing resources for client applications.
see also Web service.

session state
The process by which a Web application maintains information across a sequence of requests by the same client to the same Web application.

Simple Object Access Protocol (SOAP)
An XML-based protocol developed by Microsoft/Lotus/IBM for exchanging information between peers in a decentralized, distributed environment. SOAP allows programs on different computers to communicate independently of an operating system or platform by using the World Wide Web's HyperText Transfer Protocol (HTTP) and XML as the basis of information exchange. SOAP is now a W3C specification.
See also eXtensible Markup Language (XML), World Wide Web Consortium (W3C).

spatial data infrastructure (SDI)
A framework of technologies, policies, standards, and human resources
necessary to acquire, process, store, distribute, and improve the utilization
of geospatial data.

Standard Generalized Markup Language (SGML)
A markup language similar to XML
See also eXtensible Markup Language (XML).

Structured Query Language (SQL)
A syntax for defining and manipulating data from a relational database.
Developed by IBM in the 1970s, SQL has become an industry standard for
query languages in most relational database management systems.

Universal Description, Discovery, and Integration (UDDI)
A standard designed to permit Web services to be dynamically discovered
and invoked.

Web Feature Server (WFS)
A set of interface specifications to describe data manipulation operations on
OpenGIS simple features.

Web Map Server Specification (WMS)
A set of interface specifications that provide uniform access by Web
clients to maps rendered by map servers on the Internet. The Web Map
Server (WMS) is the result of a collaborative effort assembled by the Open
Geospatial Consortium, Inc. (OGC).

Web portal
A Web site that either assembles many online resources and links into a
single, easy-to-use product or provides search tools that help users find
information on the Web.

Web service
A software component accessible over the World Wide Web for use in other applications. Web services are built using industry standards such as XML and SOAP and thus are not dependent on any particular operating system or programming language, allowing access through a wide range of applications.

Web Service Description Language (WSDL)
The standard format for describing the methods and types of a Web service, expressed in XML.

wide area network (WAN)
A computer network that operates across public or dedicated telephone lines and connects terminals in different cities or countries.
See also local area network (LAN).

World Wide Web Consortium (W3C)
An organization that develops standards for the World Wide Web and promotes interoperability between Web technologies, such as browsers. Members from around the world contribute to standards for XML, XSL, HTML, and many other Web-based protocols.

Bernard, L., I. Kanellopoulos, A. Annoni, and P. Smits. 2005. The European geoportal—one step towards the establishment of a European Spatial Data Infrastructure. *Computers, Environment and Urban Systems* 29: 15–31.

Bishr, Y., and M. Radwan. 2000. GDI architectures. In *Geospatial data infrastructure: Concepts, cases, and good practice*, eds. R. Groot and J. McLaughlin. Oxford: Oxford University Press.

Borrebæk, M. 2004. *SOSI—Systematic Organisation of Spatial Information.* Oslo: Norwegian Mapping Authority.

Burrough, P., and I. Masser, eds. 1998. *European geographical information infrastructures: Opportunities and pitfalls.* London: Taylor & Francis.

Burrough, P., and I. Masser. 1998. International aspects of spatial data exchange. In *European geographical information infrastructures: Opportunities and pitfalls,* eds. P. Burrough and I. Masser. London: Taylor & Francis.

Croswell, P. 2000. The role of standards in support of GDI. In *Geospatial data infrastructure: Concepts, cases, and good practice,* eds. R. Groot and J. McLaughlin. Oxford: Oxford University Press.

Daukantas, P. 2003. One-Stop, two clicks. *Government Computer News.* www.gcn.com/22_22/cover/23072-1.html.

Department for Transport. 2002. Transport Direct: Phase 2 public consultation. London: Department for Transport. www.dft.gov.uk/stellent/groups/dft_about/documents/page/dft_about_022688.hcsp.

Department for Transport. 2003. Transport Direct market research programme: Findings and implications from phase 1. London: Department for Transport. www.dft.gov.uk/stellent/groups/dft_about/documents/page/dft_about_022700.hcsp.

Department for Transport. 2004. Transport Direct. London: Department for Transport. www.dft.gov.uk/stellent/groups/dft_about/documents/divisionhomepage/030779.hcsp.

Dodson, A., and J. Verouden. 2004. Globalising GIS in Shell. Proceedings 2004 ESRI User Conference.

Douglas, M. 2003. One-Stop shopping. *Government Technology.* www.govtech.net/magazine/story.php?id=62033.

ESRI. 2003. *Implementing a metadata catalog portal in a GIS network.* ESRI Whitepaper. www.esri.com/library/gisportal/pdfs/cat-portal.pdf.

ESRI. 2003. *Standards and interoperability.* ESRI Whitepaper. www.esri.com/library/whitepapers/pdfs/spatial-data-standards.pdf.

ESRI. 2003. Geospatial One-Stop portal is key to President's e-government strategy. *ArcNews Summer* 2003. www.esri.com/news/arcnews/summer03articles/geospatial-onestop.html.

ESRI. 2004. *GIS portal technology.* ESRI Whitepaper. www.esri.com/library/whitepapers/pdfs/gisportal.pdf.

ESRI. 2004. *GIS portal development workshop lectures.* Redlands: ESRI.

Evans, J. 2003. *A geospatial interoperability reference model (G.I.R.M.).* Federal Geographic Data Committee. gai.fgdc.gov/girm/v1.1.

Federal Geographic Data Committee (FGDC). 2004. *Federal Geographic Data Committee: Historical reflections—Future directions.* www.fgdc.gov/publications/fgdc_history.html.

Fisheries and Oceans Canada. 2004. *Mapster 2 tutorial.* www-heb.pac.dfo-mpo.gc.ca/ maps/tutorial/mapster_tut_e.pdf.

Fisheries and Oceans Canada. 2004. *Overview GIS internet applications.* www-heb.pac.dfo-mpo.gc.ca/maps/app_overview_e.htm.

Garie, H. 2003. Geospatial One-Stop and Hurricane Isabel—Riders on the storm. *Federal GIS connections.* Redlands: ESRI.

Goodchild, M., and J. Zhou. 2003. Finding geographic information: Collection-level metadata. *GeoInformatica* 7(2): 95–112.

References

Grady, R. 2001. Integrated facilities data system using Web and database technology. Proceedings 2001 ESRI User Conference. gis.esri.com/library/userconf/proc01/professional/papers/pap341/p341.htm.

Gregorius, T. 2003. Spatially enabling exploration and production information. SMi E&P Data and Information Management, London.

Gregorius, T. 2004. The business value of enterprise GIS in the energy industry. Proceedings Senior Executive Seminar ESRI 2004 User Conference.

Gregorius, T. 2004. Shell global GIS framework and portals. Web Enabled GIS Strategies Conference Proceedings, 2004 Sydney.

Groot, R., and J. McLaughlin, eds. 2000. *Geospatial data infrastructure: Concepts, cases, and good practice.* Oxford: Oxford University Press.

Hardy, M. 2003. Geospatial portal still elusive. FCW.com. www.fcw.com.

Hodge, G. 2001. *Metadata made simpler: A guide for libraries.* www.niso.org/news/Metadata_simpler.pdf.

Lowe, J. 2002. Finders and keepers: In search of spatial data. *Geospatial Solutions.* www.geospatial-online.com.

Maguire, D., and P. Longley 2005. The emergence of geoportals and their role in spatial data infrastructures. *Computers, Environment and Urban Systems* 29: 3–14.

Masser, I. 2005. *GIS worlds: Creating spatial data infrastructures.* Redlands: ESRI Press.

McKee, L. 2003. The spatial Web. www.opengeospatial.org/press/?page=papers.

Mellum, R. 2004. geoNorge.no—The new Norwegian geoPortal. Proceedings 2004 ESRI User Conference.

Mellum, R., and K. Kyrkjeeide. 2003. Planning information support and accessibility in Norway: AREALIS/GEOVEKST. Proceedings of Institute of Municipal Engineering of South Africa Conference, 2003 Cape Town.

Nebert, D., ed. 2004. *Developing spatial data infrastructures: SDI Cookbook version* 2.0. Reston, Va.: FGDC. www.gsdi.org.

Østensen, O. 2003. Portal developments in Norway and their role in the geospatial infrastructure. Spatial Portals Conference, University College, London.

Rhind, D. 2000. Funding an NGDI. In *Geospatial data infrastructure: Concepts, cases, and good practice,* eds. R. Groot and J. McLaughlin. Oxford: Oxford University Press.

Salgé, F. 1998. From an understanding of European GI economic activity to the reality of a European data set. In *European geographical information infrastructures: Opportunities and pitfalls,* eds. P. Burrough and I. Masser. London: Taylor & Francis.

Shultz, J. 2004. Spatially enabling public information analysis. In *Measuring up: The business case for GIS,* eds. C. Thomas and M. Ospina. Redlands: ESRI.

Smits, P., ed. 2002. *INSPIRE architecture and standards position paper.* Ispra: Joint Research Centre, European Commission.

Tait, M. 2005. Implementing geoportals: Applications of distributed GIS. *Computers, Environment and Urban Systems* 29: 33–47.

Tang, W., and J. Selwood. 2003. *Connecting our world: GIS Web services.* Redlands: ESRI Press.

Thomas, C., and M. Ospina, eds. 2004. *Measuring up: The business case for GIS.* Redlands: ESRI Press.

Thomas, D. 2004. Project of the year awards: Transport Direct. *Computing.* www.vnunet.com/analysis/1157634.

Van Eechoud, M. 1998. Legal protection of geographic information in the EU. In *European geographical information infrastructures: Opportunities and pitfalls,* eds. P. Burrough and I. Masser. London: Taylor & Francis.

Books from
ESRI Press

Advanced Spatial Analysis: The CASA Book of GIS *1-58948-073-2*
ArcGIS and the Digital City: A Hands-on Approach for Local Government *1-58948-074-0*
ArcView GIS Means Business *1-879102-51-X*
A System for Survival: GIS and Sustainable Development *1-58948-052-X*
Beyond Maps: GIS and Decision Making in Local Government *1-879102-79-X*
Cartographica Extraordinaire: The Historical Map Transformed *1-58948-044-9*
Cartographies of Disease: Maps, Mapping, and Medicine *1-58948-120-8*
Children Map the World: Selections from the Barbara Petchenik Children's World Map Competition *1-58948-125-9*
Community Geography: GIS in Action *1-58948-023-6*
Community Geography: GIS in Action Teacher's Guide *1-58948-051-1*
Confronting Catastrophe: A GIS Handbook *1-58948-040-6*
Connecting Our World: GIS Web Services *1-58948-075-9*
Conservation Geography: Case Studies in GIS, Computer Mapping, and Activism *1-58948-024-4*
Designing Better Maps: A Guide for GIS Users *1-58948-089-9*
Designing Geodatabases: Case Studies in GIS Data Modeling *1-58948-021-X*
Disaster Response: GIS for Public Safety *1-879102-88-9*
Enterprise GIS for Energy Companies *1-879102-48-X*
Extending ArcView GIS (version 3.x edition) *1-879102-05-6*
Fun with GPS *1-58948-087-2*
Getting to Know ArcGIS Desktop, Second Edition Updated for ArcGIS 9 *1-58948-083-X*
Getting to Know ArcObjects: Programming ArcGIS with VBA *1-58948-018-X*
Getting to Know ArcView GIS (version 3.x edition) *1-879102-46-3*
GIS and Land Records: The ArcGIS Parcel Data Model *1-58948-077-5*
GIS for Everyone, Third Edition *1-58948-056-2*
GIS for Health Organizations *1-879102-65-X*
GIS for Landscape Architects *1-879102-64-1*
GIS for the Urban Environment *1-58948-082-1*
GIS for Water Management in Europe *1-58948-076-7*
GIS in Public Policy: Using Geographic Information for More Effective Government *1-879102-66-8*
GIS in Schools *1-879102-85-4*
GIS in Telecommunications *1-879102-86-2*
GIS Means Business, Volume II *1-58948-033-3*
GIS Tutorial: Workbook for ArcView 9 *1-58948-127-5*
GIS, Spatial Analysis, and Modeling *1-58948-130-5*
GIS Worlds: Creating Spatial Data Infrastructures *1-58948-122-4*
Hydrologic and Hydraulic Modeling Support with Geographic Information Systems *1-879102-80-3*
Integrating GIS and the Global Positioning System *1-879102-81-1*
Making Community Connections: The Orton Family Foundation Community Mapping Program *1-58948-071-6*
Managing Natural Resources with GIS *1-879102-53-6*
Mapping Census 2000: The Geography of U.S. Diversity *1-58948-014-7*
Mapping Our World: GIS Lessons for Educators, ArcView GIS 3.x Edition *1-58948-022-8*
Mapping Our World: GIS Lessons for Educators, ArcGIS Desktop Edition *1-58948-121-6*
Mapping the Future of America's National Parks: Stewardship through Geographic Information Systems *1-58948-080-5*
Mapping the News: Case Studies in GIS and Journalism *1-58948-072-4*
Marine Geography: GIS for the Oceans and Seas *1-58948-045-7*
Measuring Up: The Business Case for GIS *1-58948-088-0*
Modeling Our World: The ESRI Guide to Geodatabase Design *1-879102-62-5*
Past Time, Past Place: GIS for History *1-58948-032-5*

Continued on next page

When ordering, please mention book title and ISBN (number that follows each title)

Books from ESRI Press *(continued)*

Planning Support Systems: Integrating Geographic Information Systems, Models, and Visualization Tools *1-58948-011-2*
Remote Sensing for GIS Managers *1-58948-081-3*
Salton Sea Atlas *1-58948-043-0*
Spatial Portals: Gateways to Geographic Information *1-58948-131-3*
The ESRI Guide to GIS Analysis, Volume 1: Geographic Patterns and Relationships *1-879102-06-4*
The ESRI Guide to GIS Analysis, Volume 2: Spatial Measurements and Statistics *1-58948-116-X*
Think Globally, Act Regionally: GIS and Data Visualization for Social Science and Public Policy Research *1-58948-124-0*
Thinking About GIS: Geographic Information System Planning for Managers (paperback edition) *1-58948-119-4*
Transportation GIS *1-879102-47-1*
Undersea with GIS *1-58948-016-3*
Unlocking the Census with GIS *1-58948-113-5*
Zeroing In: Geographic Information Systems at Work in the Community *1-879102-50-1*

Forthcoming titles from ESRI Press
Arc Hydro: GIS for Water Resources, Second Edition *1-58948-126-7*
A to Z GIS: An Illustrated Dictionary of Geographic Information Systems *1-58948-140-2*
Charting the Unknown: How Computer Mapping at Harvard Became GIS *1-58948-118-6*
Finding Your Customers: GIS for Retail Management *1-58948-123-2*
GIS for Environmental Management *1-58948-142-9*
GIS for the Urban Environment *1-58948-082-1*
GIS Methods for Urban Analysis *1-58948-143-7*
The GIS Guide for Local Government Officials *1-58948-141-0*

Ask for ESRI Press titles at your local bookstore or order by calling 1-800-447-9778. You can also shop online at www.esri.com/esripress. Outside the United States, contact your local ESRI distributor.

ESRI Press titles are distributed to the trade by the following:

In North America, South America, Asia, and Australia:
Independent Publishers Group (IPG)
Telephone (United States): 1-800-888-4741 • Telephone (international): 312-337-0747
E-mail: frontdesk@ipgbook.com

In the United Kingdom, Europe, and the Middle East:
Transatlantic Publishers Group Ltd.
Telephone: 44 20 8849 8013 • Fax: 44 20 8849 5556 • E-mail: transatlantic.publishers@regusnet.com

ESRI Press • 380 New York Street • Redlands, California 92373-8100 • www.esri.com/esripress